Behoref Hayamim
In the Winter of Life

Reconstructionist Rabbinical College
Center for Jewish Ethics

WYNCOTE, PENNSYLVANIA
2002/5761

Beḥoref Hayamim
In the Winter of Life

A Values-Based
Jewish Guide
for Decision Making
at the End of Life

Reconstructionist Rabbinical College Press
Wyncote, Pennsylvania

Design by Adrianne Onderdonk Dudden
Composition by Duke & Company

Library of Congress Cataloging-in-Publication Data
Behoref hayamim = In the winter of life : a values-based Jewish guide
for decision-making at the end of life / Reconstructionist Rabbinical College,
Center for Jewish Ethics.
p. cm.
Includes bibliographical references and index.
ISBN 0-938945-06-8
1. Death—Religious aspects—Judaism. 2. Death—Moral and ethical aspects.
3. Terminal care—Religious aspects—Judaism. 4. Critically ill—Legal status,
laws, etc. (Jewish law) 5. Ethics, Jewish. I. Title: In the winter of life.
II. Reconstructionist Rabbinical College (Wyncote, Pa.). Center for Jewish Ethics.
BM635.4 .B44 2002
296.3'3—dc21
2002000668

*We are grateful to those whose support
made this publication possible:*

The Nathan Cummings Foundation
Healthcare Foundation of New Jersey
Levin-Lieber Family Program in Jewish Ethics
Whizin Foundation

ADVISORY BOARD

CONTENTS

ACKNOWLEDGMENTS

This project was conceptualized by Dawn Robinson Rose and David Teutsch, then developed into a proposal by Deborah Waxman. Paul Root Wolpe, Bill Kavesh and Dawn Rose selected authors. Andrea Kydd and Rachel Cowan, program directors of the Nathan Cummings Foundation, played critical roles in launching the project. Dan Ehrenkrantz, Jules Titelbaum, and Alan Lippman guided and encouraged the project's relationship with the Healthcare Foundation of New Jersey. Bruce Whizin and Dan Levin have been generous supporters of the Center for Jewish Ethics at the Reconstructionist Rabbinical College.

The project was guided by a thoughtful and talented Advisory Board, and the chapters were written by gifted, experienced experts. David Teutsch and Deborah Waxman did the editing.

Jeremy Schwartz helped with research. Moti Rieber and Marilyn Silverstein did copy-editing. Diane Schwartz prepared the manuscript for publication. Christopher Bugbee assisted with production of the book, which owes its artful design to the sure hand and discerning eye of Adrianne Onderdonk Dudden.

Elliot N. Dorff

PREFACE

Refuat hanefesh urefuat haguf—healing of the spirit and healing of the body. This phrase from the traditional prayer for the sick summarizes the content and the approach of this important anthology of articles. Neither body nor soul exists without the other; they continually interact and influence each other. As a result, while one's body can be healed while one's soul is still at wit's end or depressed, and conversely, while one's spirit can be healed even if one's body cannot be, we must always pay attention to both aspects of our being and to the significant ways in which they affect each other.

Center for Jewish Ethics · Reconstructionist Rabbinical College

This very Jewish approach to human existence may seem obvious to contemporary North Americans, but it was not at all obvious to most peoples of the past and is still not obvious to many people in the present. In Western culture beginning with Plato, there is a sharp dichotomy between body and mind, with the body depicted as "the prison house" of the mind. Since the body comes into existence and leaves it, and since it is only the mind that can grasp abstract concepts and thus achieve that which is distinctly human, the body has been seen as clearly inferior to the mind in most of Western thought. In fact, "the mind–body problem" has been a stock issue in Western philosophy—that is, since the body and mind are so different from each other, how can they be connected altogether?

Similarly, in classical Christian thought, a sharp dichotomy exists between body and soul. According to Paul in the New Testament's *Letter to the Romans,* the body leads the soul to sin. The optimal life, therefore, is lived by those who suppress the body in order to cultivate the soul—nuns, priests, and monks.

While classical Jewish sources recognize the difference between our body and soul, they maintain that God has interwoven them to make each dependent on the other. This parable states that clearly:

> Antoninus said to Rabbi (Judah, the President, or "Prince," of the Sanhedrin), "The body and soul could exonerate themselves from judgment. How is this so? The body could say, 'The soul sinned, for from the day that it separated from me, lo, I am like a silent stone in the grave!' And the soul could say, 'The body is the sinner, for from the day that I separated from it, lo, I fly like a bird.'"
>
> Rabbi [Judah] answered him, "I will tell you a parable. What is the matter like? It is like a king of flesh and blood who

had a beautiful orchard, and there were in it lovely ripe fruit. He placed two guardians over it, one a cripple and the other blind. Said the cripple to the blind man, 'I see beautiful ripe fruit in the orchard. Come and carry me, and we will bring and eat them.' The cripple rode on the back of the blind man, and they brought and ate them. After a while the owner of the orchard came and said to them, 'Where is my lovely fruit?' The cripple answered, 'Do I have legs to go?' The blind man answered, 'Do I have eyes to see?' What did the owner do? He placed the cripple on the back of the blind man and judged them as one. So also the Holy Blessed One brings the soul and throws it into the body and judges them as one."[1]

Not only is this fundamental integration manifest in God's ultimate, divine judgment of each of us; it is also the rabbinic recipe for life. Although the rabbis emphasized the importance of studying and following the Torah, even placing it on a par with all of the rest of the commandments,[2] they nonetheless believed that the life of the soul or mind by itself is not good, that it can indeed be the source of sin:

An excellent thing is the study of Torah combined with some worldly occupation, for the labor demanded by both of them causes sinful inclinations to be forgotten. All study of Torah without work must, in the end, be futile and become the cause of sin.[3]

Thus, while the rabbis considered it a privilege to be able to study Torah, they themselves—or at least most of them—earned their livelihood through bodily work, and they also valued the hard labor of the field worker who spends little time in the study of Torah:

A favorite saying of the rabbis of Yavneh was: I am God's creature, and my fellow [who works in the field and is not a student]
is God's creature. My work is in the town, and his work is in
the country. I rise early for my work, and he rises early for his
work. Just as he does not presume to do my work, so I do not
presume to do his work. Will you say, I do much [in the study
of Torah] and he does little? We have learned: One may do
much or one may do little; it is all one, provided that the person's heart is directed to Heaven.[4]

So if God judges us as whole human beings, integrating body
and spirit, and if we are to appreciate people's contributions of both
mind and body and seek to exercise both in our lives, it is clearly
important to pay attention to both in caring for the ill. That is
the clear message of these Jewish sources, and it is the clear import
of the mention of both in the traditional Jewish prayer for healing.

This book is therefore very Jewish in continually reemphasizing the integration of healing of the body with healing of the
soul. It contains important information on the common medical
questions that families face at the end of life—all in language
understandable to people not trained in medicine. At the same
time, it gives people insights into what the spirit needs at such
times and how to provide it, while not neglecting one's own
body or spirit in the process. For these matters of content alone
this book is well worth the read.

But the authors and publisher had a methodological point
in mind as well. In the second paragraph of the very first essay,
Dr. David Teutsch makes it clear that all the essays presume a
"post-halakhic" methodology

because we live in a post-halakhic world, a world where Jewish
law cannot be enforced. Obligations, moral decisions, and

spiritual discipline exist without the enforcement of a functioning Jewish legal system. This in turn has disrupted the adaptive mechanisms of *halakha*. Thus we take *halakha* seriously as a source and resource that can shape expectations while not necessarily seeing ourselves as bound by inherited claims of obligation. Therefore . . . the *Guide* is designed to provide insights, arguments, and approaches that can be used by the individual decision-maker or groups of decision-makers according to their own lights. . . .

This methodology is specifically invoked several times in the volume by various authors—Paul Root Wolpe and Richard Hirsh—and it is assumed by virtually all of the other authors as well.

As a Conservative rabbi, I do not share that methodology. For reasons that I have discussed elsewhere,[5] I think that a proper legal methodology is best suited to address contemporary moral issues in a distinctly Jewish way. This book, though, is an excellent display of what responsible, Jewish decision making should look like outside its classical legal frame. Moreover, even with this serious methodological difference, I am happily surprised to find that I agree with much of the advice contained in this volume. That is a testament to the authors' sincere efforts to make this a deeply Jewish book, informing readers of some important aspects of modern medicine while applying Jewish concepts and values to the issues that it poses.

Refuat hanefesh urefuat haguf—healing of soul and healing of body. I am writing this Preface just a few weeks after the terrorist attacks on the World Trade Center in New York and the Pentagon in Washington, D.C. People always need healing of soul and body; we are especially cognizant of those needs at times of national tragedies like this one. May this book help us all to bring both these great gifts of God to so many in our world who sorely need them.

University of Judaism
Los Angeles, CA
September 30, 2001

Beḥoref Hayamim
In the Winter of Life

David Teutsch

1

INTRODUCTION:
JEWISH VALUES AND DECISION MAKING

The challenges faced by people at the end of life are myriad
and complex. Those challenges have components that are psychological, physical, medical, emotional, and familial. Often these
challenges are spiritual as well. In this context, people often
look to Jewish tradition for guidance. Most American Jews do
not consider themselves to be bound by *halakha* (Jewish law).
Instead, they would like to draw on the values, experiences and
insights of Jewish tradition while forming their own responses
to situations that are often made complex by medical advances,

high technology, distance, and a host of other factors. This *Guide* is meant to provide help for individuals, families, and professionals who would like guidance that draws on Jewish resources.

While this *Guide* is meant to serve all who find its approach to Jewish living helpful, its position is post-halakhic because we live in a post-halakhic world, a world where Jewish law cannot be enforced. Obligations, moral decisions, and spiritual discipline exist without the enforcement of a functioning Jewish legal system. This in turn has disrupted the adaptive mechanisms of *halakha*. Thus we take *halakha* seriously as a source and resource that can shape expectations while not necessarily seeing ourselves as bound by inherited claims of obligation. Therefore the choices advocated in this *Guide* are not monolithic. The *Guide* is designed to provide insights, arguments, and approaches that can be used by the individual decision maker or groups of decision makers according to their own lights. Thus this *Guide* assumes that thoughtful individuals and groups can handle complexity and will of necessity reach their own conclusions.

Jewish decision making through the ages reflected the fact that Jews lived in an organic Jewish community. While individuals had substantial autonomy in many areas, their thinking and decisions were profoundly shaped by their Jewish communities. The organic community was shattered by modernity and the emergence of nations granting secular citizenship.

Today few Jews outside Israel live primarily in Jewish community. Studying the issues and approaches discussed in this volume in congregational or professional settings can help to provide group reflection and insight. That is as close as most of us can come to participating in a communal milieu that shapes our values and decisions. Absent such conversation, our intuitions are shaped by the mass media. Self-conscious exploration of values and attitudes and their implications gives us more control over our decisions.

This volume cites stories and opinions from a variety of Jewish sources. None of these is understood as authoritative by itself, and some even contradict each other. They are cited to demonstrate inherited attitudes and practices worthy of our consideration and evaluation rather than to dictate decisions on outcomes.

In this volume, the term *mitzva* is used to refer to a moral obligation. While often mistranslated as "good deed," *mitzva* literally means "commandment." Such a use carries both certain theological claims (since commandment implies a Commander) and politico-social ones *(halakha* being the source of definitions of *mitzvot).* In this volume the term is used to mean a moral imperative that emerges from Jewish culture. Use of *mitzva* here does not assume either a commitment to *halakha* or a particular theology. In any case, most of this *Guide* is not concerned with clear imperatives. It is meant to address areas of conduct where we must make often difficult choices.

This *Guide* stands solidly within a tradition of value-based decision making. Such decision making follows a method that many people who use this *Guide* may find helpful. Its steps can be summarized as follows:

1 Determine facts, alternative actions and their outcomes, and relevant beliefs and values.

2 Examine relevant scientific and social-scientific approaches to understanding these.

3 Consider the historical and contemporary context, includ-ing the history and rationales of Jewish practice.

4 Look for norms that might exclude some actions.

5 Weigh the relevant attitudes, beliefs, and values.

6 Formulate decision alternatives.

7 Seek consensus (if a group is deciding).

8 Make the decision.

These steps in decision making will necessarily be shaped in very different ways depending upon the issues to which they are applied. Some of those issues are put in a context of advanced technology, diagnosis, and treatment and must therefore be considered alongside a substantial amount of scientific data. Some of them will be about how to use technology or when to stop. Some of them will be about how to deal with pain and suffering. Some will be about the circumstances under which care should be given, and some will be concerned with dying, death, and the decisions that must be made after death. While each of these decisions will be shaped by differing circumstances and medical information, all of them must sooner or later involve the application of basic values. Since many of these will come up repeatedly in the chapters that follow, the values and ideas that are particularly pertinent to much of this discussion are summarized below:

Ahava (Love). The gift of love—from parent to child, between lovers and friends, teachers and students—is a central source of joy, nurture and growth, bringing much of what gives life its meaning. Jewish tradition portrays God as the ultimate source of love, embodied in Creation, in Torah and in relationships. Valuing love involves making efforts to sustain and protect loving relationships.

Beriyut (Health and wellness). Jewish tradition values the body and good health, supporting measures to protect them. Taking pleasure in the senses and avoiding destructive behavior reflect this value, as does the pursuit of spiritual and emotional health. The value of *beriyut* needs to be applied not only to a patient seeking health, but also to the caregivers who must be conscious of the need to protect their health even as they provide the care that is needed.

B'tzelem Elohim (Human beings are created in the image of God.). Because we see ourselves as having a spark of the divine within, we understand every person has infinite worth; therefore, no human being should be treated merely as an object, and we should always attempt to see the humanity in those we encounter. This attitude, drawn from Genesis 1:26, underlies many Jewish values.

Eyt lamut (Time to die). While premature death is to be avoided wherever possible, Jewish tradition acknowledges that we are all bound to die. Having made oneself ready at the end of life makes it possible to die in a way that preserves human dignity. The central issue for anyone struggling with the end of life is to consider how to create the conditions for a good death and to know when the time has come for that inevitable result.

Goses (One certain to die). Jewish tradition recognizes a category of persons certain not to recover from fatal illness known as *t'refa*. Once the person is inevitably slipping toward death and has only a short time to live, that person is a *goses*, viewed as no longer fully alive. The categories of *t'refa* and *goses* make it possible to consider how to treat those at the end of life in a way somewhat different from those who are ill but not yet in the very final stages of life.

Ḥesed (Covenantal caring). The lovingkindness in action that we bring to members of our communities and our families is the embodiment of love concretely expressed whether we are actually feeling love at any given moment or not. Caring for each other is part of what makes us fully human.

Kedusha (Holiness). Leviticus tells us that God is absolutely holy and that the times, places, and actions that bring us closer to God are holy as well. Jewish observance is intended to help us become more holy, more fully in touch with the Divine within us and in the world. *Kedusha* has a root meaning of separate, dedicated, or set apart. Particularly in an overwhelmingly secular society, efforts to follow a path of holiness can create life-rhythms that to some extent set one apart from others. We should attempt to maximize the holiness with which we look at the situation of those who are ill and respond to them, conscious that our relationships too can reflect holiness.

K'vod habriyot (Human dignity). Created *b'tzelem Elohim,* in the image of God, we can see the spark of the Divine in each other. In recognizing that each human face is in part a face of the Divine, we recognize that we are bound to respect the dignity of each human being and act in a way consistent with that dignity. Those who are ill, impaired, or otherwise dependent upon us deserve to be treated in a way that preserves their dignity to the fullest extent possible in every situation.

Ladonay ha'aretz umelo'o (The earth and all that is in it belong to God [Psalms 24:1].). We are the beneficiaries of Creation and its stewards. Human beings do not ultimately own what is theirs in the world; it is on loan to us, and we are responsible for doing with it what we believe its Owner would will. This key idea underlies Jewish social ethics.

Mitzva (Obligation). Jewish tradition teaches that God gave the 613 *mitzvot* in the Torah. While we do not believe that each obligation we have was individually formulated for us by God and we realize that obligations inevitably change over time, we recognize that community can only exist if there are rules that community members follow. Doing what I believe is the right thing simply because it is right helps to create an inner life that is clear as well as interpersonal bonds that are reliable. Some *mitzvot* serve as pathways connecting us to our community and our people, to our highest values, to humanity and to God. Caring for those who are ill is a *mitzva*.

Pikuaḥ nefesh (Saving a life). In Jewish tradition, saving a life takes precedence over almost anything else. In an earlier generation, preserving life was seen as paramount over all other medical goals. In our time, our ability to preserve life is much greater. Therefore, the balancing of this value with such other values as the quality of life has recently made the application of the value of *pikuaḥ nefesh* much more challenging.

Rahmanut (Compassion/mercy). Empathy for those who are less fortunate results in caring action that can involve the emotional, physical, and economic realms. Everyone is less fortunate in some way, and all human beings are vulnerable. We need to have compassion for ourselves and others, especially those suffering from emotional, spiritual, physical, and financial difficulties. The Hebrew root of the word *rahmanut* is *reḥem,* womb, which implies a deep and abiding love. Everyone is in need of our caring and compassion. Those who are dying and their loved ones are particularly in need of *rahmanut*.

Refua (Healing). The healing of body *(refuat haguf)* and of mind and spirit *(refuat hanefesh)* are not only the subject of prayer;

they are also states of being that we can achieve by human caring. Healing in this sense not only refers to the physician's task of utilizing the best medical interventions; rather, it refers to those actions that bring a sense of well-being into the life of the individual. This is possible when human beings receive the nurture, affection, and support that they need in order to move toward a state of spiritual and emotional well-being. Healing is possible even for a person who is dying.

Sh'lom bayit (Peace in the family). Preserving the harmony in familial relationships is a critical part of guaranteeing family stability. Those who share their lives through family should be honored, nurtured, and loved by each other. When this nurturing is present, it allows the individuals in the family to blossom. When it is absent because of abuse or violence or acts of humiliation or the failure to grant the dignity of other family members, *sh'lom bayit* is impossible. Helping family members to work through disagreements in a constructive way and to support each other's dignity is critical to the lives of the members of the family.

Sh'mirat haguf (Guarding the body). Every individual has an obligation to look out for his or her own health. By eating well, getting sufficient sleep, getting enough exercise, and obtaining sufficient medical treatment, people can preserve the gift of their bodies, which are the repositories for their minds as well. The obligation of *sh'mirat haguf* pertains both to caregivers and to patients—in fact, to everyone who has the gift of life.

Yirat shamayim (Reverence for God). The individual's personal preferences are not the ultimate arbiter of ethics in the world. Reverence for God suggests that we are responsible for standards of justice and holiness that are beyond each individual. We seek to be aware of that greater presence in our lives and to be guided by it, aware that the human intellect and the human spirit are limited, and that we need to seek guidance that goes beyond the individual.

This list of values is not an exhaustive one, and the reader will find additional values utilized by the authors of this volume. The *Guide* provides an overview of medical technologies and issues raised by them, the challenges when one knows about the diagnosis of an illness, basic choices faced by a decision maker, how we approach pain and suffering, end-of-life care and hospice, and death and dying. Experts in each of these fields— physicians, ethicists, and chaplaincy experts—have produced these chapters. The guidance they provide should enrich readers' thinking and help them to apply a Jewish moral perspective to end-of-life decision making.

William Kavesh

2

TAKING CONTROL OF DIFFICULT DECISIONS

Planning Barriers and Incentives

Most people do not plan for end–of–life decision making. The reasons for this are complex. Some people feel that the physician is in control of things and will take care of whatever is necessary. Others are overwhelmed by the technical aspects of ventilators (breathing machines) and other paraphernalia. The notion of trying to anticipate what will happen at the end of life may appear to have a certain element of interfering with God's work

Center for Jewish Ethics · Reconstructionist Rabbinical College

or hastening the arrival of the *"malakh hamavet"* (the angel of death). Perhaps related to this is the deeply rooted idea that something bad could not happen at a young age. Many people acknowledge the studies that show that teenagers have a sense of invincibility that may interfere with safe behavior. However, a 40 year old (or 70 year old) may also feel that there is little reason to deal with issues that are supposed to arise years down the line.

Furthermore, people may have unpleasant associations with end-of-life situations involving relatives, and may not want to unearth the inevitable painful memories that arise. Closely related is the notion harbored by some children that it is best to spare their older relative or friend the pain and anxiety which may arise from confronting death and disability. This perspective may be reinforced by some Jewish thinking on this subject that truth-telling may sap a person's will to live. Families that do not communicate effectively about difficult issues may be particularly drawn to this mechanism of denial. Finally, recent studies demonstrate that no matter what advance planning has gone on, a significant percentage of people are resuscitated even though they indicated they did not want that. Some people, perhaps feeling limited capacity to influence events on a cosmic or mundane level, may feel that no matter what they say, it won't affect the outcome, so avoiding the issue may be the easiest approach.

From a Jewish perspective, there are many reasons why planning for life's inevitable decline is appropriate and important. Judaism has always considered attention to the body and its care of paramount importance. This notion may be exemplified by the midrashic tale about Hillel: When he had finished the lesson with his pupils, he accompanied them part of the way. They said to him, "Master, where are you going?" "To perform a religious duty." "Which religious duty?" "To bathe in the bath house."

"Is that a religious duty?" He answered them: "If somebody is appointed to scrape and clean the statues of the king that are set up in the theaters and circuses, is paid to do the work, and furthermore associates with the nobility, how much more so should I, who am created in the divine image and likeness, take care of my body!"[6]

This idea that we are created *b'tzelem Elohim,* in the image of God, is a traditional notion that continues to be emphasized by liberal Jewish thinkers today.[7] However a modern Jew chooses to interpret the concept of being created in God's image, the idea that we should value our bodies and need to plan for their care is well-rooted in Jewish thinking.

Several practical consequences derive from the concept of *tzelem Elohim.* First, preventive medicine is an important ideal. Maimonides emphasizes that we should engage in moderate and healthy behavior that forestalls the onset of disease wherever possible.[8] Thus, healthy eating, exercise and health screening for potentially preventable illnesses, such as various cancers, are Jewish imperatives. We do not subscribe to the notion that disease comes from God and there is therefore nothing that we can or should do to forestall the workings of the Divine, whether conceived of as outside or inside this world. Rather, we tend to rely on the ideas expressed in the rabbinic dicta that God provides medical insights to humankind and that seeking out medical attention is an appropriate corollary to this notion. Thus, the Talmud maintains that it is forbidden to live in a city where there is no physician.[9] The rabbis traced this idea back to Exodus 21:18–19, which indicates that it is the obligation of a person who injures another to "pay for his idleness and cure." The traditional interpretation is that he shall pay the doctor's bill.

Taking this Jewish interventionist stance into account, when is it appropriate to begin to take control of planning for the end of life? One form of advance planning common in Jewish history is the ethical will. In ethical wills the authors address the moral legacy they wish to leave their families. A mix of insight and instruction, ethical wills are a wonderful legacy to leave behind. They illustrate the caring that advance planning embodies. Ethical wills sometimes include instructions regarding funerals and mourning. In our time a similar document might well provide guidance regarding care during a debilitating illness, since prolonged medical care is a relatively recent phenomenon.

This *Guide* is primarily written for caregivers and individuals who may have to assist in decision making (proxies), but given medical advances and Jewish attitudes toward medical care, decision making ought to start before an illness strikes. At that point, there is usually no caregiver or proxy. The responsibility then falls upon the individual to initiate the process, although some physicians have begun to urge their patients to think about these issues well in advance of the onset of an illness. Most state motor vehicle departments now ask drivers to indicate for their drivers' licenses whether they want to donate organs in case of a fatal accident. It could be argued that Jewish professionals ought to make advance health planning part of their guidance for those with whom they interact.

What situations require advance planning? Many illnesses give plenty of warning that life may draw to a premature close. Dementias—in which there is a gradual loss of memory, language skills, and other functions—usually progress for many years. Judgment is often preserved early on. Cancer usually gives a warning well before end-of-life issues need to be addressed. AIDS is now a chronic illness, and most people can anticipate its complications for many years. Heart failure, in which there may be a progressive loss of the ability to walk and do other functions without severe shortness of breath, is often, though not always, protracted over several years. Neurological disorders such as spinal-cord injuries and ALS (Lou Gehrig's disease) result in an acute or progressive loss of muscular function that often allows much time for reflection. On the other hand, catastrophic illness can come with no warning upon a person who has apparently been healthy until then. A stroke can abruptly cut off a person's ability to communicate with others and make care wishes known. The rabbis picked age 40 as a key transition point in life, whether for venturing into the dangerous waters of Jewish mysticism, or for reaching the age of understanding.[10] It also begins the decade in which deaths due to cardiovascular disease and cancer begin to make their presence known among our peers. It is probably a good time for all of us to begin to think about what we would do if the unexpected strikes and to consider creating an advance directive, a written document of health-care preferences to be carried out when a person is no longer capable of making decisions.

Key Issues in the Planning Process

One of the key ethical underpinnings of the modern American health system is the notion of autonomy. A person has the right to make the ultimate decisions about his or her medical care. Autonomy in health-care decision making is really a late 20th-century phenomenon. There was a time when the physician made most health-care decisions with little input from the patient, and some people still prefer to ask their physician to make important decisions for them. However, the culture of medicine, either because of philosophical commitment or fear of lawsuits, has changed to the point where patients and their families/surrogates are usually empowered/required to authorize most key health-care interventions. This process is not without its trauma. Some people are put in the position of making far-reaching decisions with limited understanding of the complex technical details or other implications of what they sign. Other families may have deep divisions or ambivalence among different members about the correct way to go, and the decision can come back to haunt them if the outcome of the decision turns out to be a bad one.

The notion of autonomy is not about to be overturned, but it is undergoing some rethinking in liberal Jewish circles. Not long ago, traditional Jews made most important decisions after consulting a rabbi, who would decide for them in accord with the applicable halakhic (legal) tradition. This tradition might grant some autonomy—for example, a pregnant woman was allowed to eat whatever she wanted even if it was thought to potentially harm the fetus—but generally has been thought of as a relatively hierarchical system.[11] As we shall see, even Orthodoxy permits far more autonomy in the late 20th century than might be expected. But the important thing for liberal Jews is that, based on a religious imperative, contemporary Jewish thinkers also suggest that there are limits to autonomy. This liberal idea of limiting autonomy originates in the objections that most Jewish thinkers have toward assisted suicide. The philosophic basis for this revulsion is the idea that we are all created *b'tzelem Elohim,* in the image of God. Many rabbis regard assisted suicide as an affront to this notion. Some Reform thinkers use traditional language in suggesting that life is a gift from God and God will decide when life shall end.[12] Reconstructionists arrive at the same conclusion from a somewhat different perspective. They argue that human beings have the Divine in them and thereby participate in the infinite worth of the Divine. Assisted suicide debases this conception of humanity. Secular Jews who believe in the ultimate worth of human life might well reach the same conclusion for different reasons.

Advance planning considers how to maximize the quantity and quality of life. Sometimes there is difficulty in balancing between the two. One major consideration in making end-of-life medical decisions is what the balance should be. The traditional Jewish emphasis on quantity of life did not anticipate the current array of medical interventions, leading contemporary Jewish medical ethics to consider how to respond. All of these broad questions provide part of the context for contemporary medical planning and decision making.

We conclude this section with one final caveat. As we shall see, Jewish opposition to assisted suicide does not mean acceptance of pain or suffering. Rather, it emphasizes the high value accorded to human life across the Jewish spectrum. Control of pain is an essential element in maintaining the value of human life.

Beginning the Decision-making Process

Given a broad, but not unlimited, mandate for autonomy of the individual, who, then, should participate in discussions around issues that involve making difficult decisions? In keeping with the ideas expressed above, it is fair to say that a normative Jewish perspective generally includes the idea that difficult decisions are best made in community. In an Orthodox setting, the rabbi may represent the community. In more liberal settings, the rabbi may also provide guidance, but the degree of authority attributed to the rabbi's input may vary. Most people find it helpful to consult family, close friends, and counselors.

Many people who are part of close-knit groups such as havurot (small religious communities or synagogue groups) may find that there are members with specialized knowledge or previous experiences that may provide helpful guidance. The doctor also should be a primary source of information. One of the key functions that a doctor, rabbi or other professional counselor may play is to advocate for the patient who is getting suggestions from family or others that are motivated by self-interest or psychological conflict. This aspect of decision making is discussed further in Chapter Five.

Legal Issues. Many people find themselves bogged down by the confusing terminology which is used in dealing with healthcare decision making. Four terms recur over and over again: decision-making capacity, durable power of attorney, competency, and guardianship. All of these involve situations where a person may be transferring certain decision-making rights to others, but there is a big difference between the first two, which do not involve a court, and the last two, which require court intervention.

Decision-making capacity is a determination which is made by a professional, usually a physician, that a person is in possession of a set of values and goals, can communicate and understand information, and can reason and deliberate about his/her choices.[13] In some states, a second licensed practitioner (a psychologist or other professional) may also be required to participate in this decision.[14] The assessment of decision-making capacity must precede any other steps to transfer responsibility for health-care decisions to another person.

If the individual is deemed to be in possession of decision-making capacity, the person then may execute a durable power of attorney for health care. A power of attorney is a document that authorizes another person, usually a relative, to make decisions for the person. If the person loses decision-making capacity, a power of attorney may no longer be valid. A "durable" power of attorney endures even when the individual no longer possesses decision-making capacity. A durable power of attorney for health care authorizes the other person to make decisions about health-care issues. It may, or may not, include authorization for the other person to make decisions about other matters, such as financial issues. The advantage of executing a durable power of attorney is that it is much less expensive and time-consuming than going to court. In theory, there is a potential for abuse since it only has to be witnessed to be valid, and an unscrupulous relative might exert undue influence on a person to sign over authority. However, this does not appear to be a significant problem in the authors' experience. If a health-care provider, or other relevant individual, feels that the person with the power of attorney is abusing the authority, there is always the option to go to a court and seek guardianship.

Competency is "the global ability to participate in the full range of daily transactions of society."[15] Competency is a legal status. A person is deemed competent until a court determines that the person is incompetent. In theory, a person who has been determined to have lost decision-making capacity still remains competent, but as a practical matter, someone else will be making decisions for the person unless there is another person willing to go to court to challenge this. A judge determines if a person is competent by calling a hearing in which the interested parties participate. A physician and one or more other professionals may be called to testify. Usually a psychiatric opinion is included in the reports to the court.

Once a person is deemed incompetent, the judge will appoint a guardian, an individual who is given broad authority to make decisions for the person, typically including financial matters and all health matters, including decisions about surgery, use of respirators, resuscitation, feeding tubes, and so on. The guardian must provide the court with regular updates on the incompetent individual's status, and the judge can question the guardian's decisions if the judge has a concern or an individual petitions the court to review what the guardian has done. Guardianship is a substantial responsibility. If an interested relative is not willing to become the guardian, courts may have difficulty finding a person to take on the task. Social-service organizations that used to provide individuals to take on this role are less and less willing to do so now that their financial resources are limited in the current health-care environment. It is best to use the mechanism of the durable power of attorney when possible. Once a person loses decision-making capacity, however, the time for execution of a durable power of attorney for health care has passed, and guardianship may be the only alternative.

When the patient is temporarily or permanently incompetent and there is no durable power of attorney, hospitals can go to court and get a temporary guardianship, but this can delay matters. If everyone seems to be looking out for the best interests of the person involved, using the person with the power of attorney is often the best route. This is probably still a reasonable course of action even if it is suspected that the patient may have signed it when s/he wasn't completely capable of sorting out nuances but seems to trust the person with the power of attorney. As a practical matter, hospitals find it so cumbersome that they rarely go to court seeking a guardianship unless the patient has no identifiable relatives or friends. Even in the absence of a durable power of attorney, most hospitals will take the signature of a relative or close friend to authorize a necessary procedure, as long as there is no one else present who questions it.

Jewish Views of Decision-making Capacity.
Judaism has several terms to describe a person who has lost his/her wits. The most common of these is *shoteh*. The *shoteh* is defined slightly differently in different places in the Talmud, but all the definitions are based on the person's behavior. For example, one talmudic

source defines a *shoteh* as a person who takes off his clothes in public, sleeps in the cemetery, or engages in other forms of bizarre behavior. From a Jewish perspective a *shoteh* would be incompetent. As a practical matter, secular laws obtain in these situations.

Advance Directives

Advance directives are an extension of the concept of autonomy. If individuals have the ultimate say as to how their health-care

---

PRACTICAL ADVICE:
Creating a power of attorney for health care.

- Ask your local hospital or bar association for the proper forms.

- Talk to the doctor to determine that the person has decision-making capacity.

- Talk to family members to make sure everyone understands what is about to happen and doesn't object.

- If there is a problem designating one person with the authority, try to talk it through together.

- If the conflict remains, ask a rabbi, doctor, or other knowledgeable professional to help.

- If there is still a problem, the person with power of attorney may simply have to accept that the disagreements may not be fully resolved and proceed.

- Fill out the forms together and have them notarized.

- Make several copies for doctors, a lawyer, and family.

---

needs should be met, then surely they ought to be able to plan for situations in which they may not be able to express their wishes. After all, we write wills to determine what will happen to our property after we die. If people can respect a will, they ought to be able to respect what some call a living will.

There are differences between a will and an advance directive. It is fairly straightforward to define what you want to happen to your property. There are not that many places where it is likely to go, and they can be defined fairly precisely. When it comes to health status, things can be very ambiguous. Some advance directives provide a long list of things that you may or may not want done in the event that your health deteriorates to a certain degree. For example, a typical list includes the option of indicating whether or not to have surgery once you reach a certain state of deterioration—which could be anything from an irreversible coma to a dementia to a gradual loss of muscle function as in ALS, or advanced cancer, or heart or respiratory failure. The list, in fact, could be a lot longer. But the important thing is that if you check off that you don't want surgery, period, what happens in the situation where you develop circulatory problems in a toe and painful gangrene develops? If the toe is amputated, a very brief operation, the pain is relieved. If not, you end up on high doses of pain-controlling medications, often requiring shots or intravenous administration. These may control the pain some or much of the time, depending on how well versed the physician is in pain control, as the infection gradually spreads over a period of weeks or longer until the end comes.

There are many other scenarios that can happen with checklists, where a person simply cannot anticipate the possible situations that might arise. This is why many ethicists recommend that an advance directive should not consist simply of a set of items to be checked off. Rather, it should include two other key items: a list of values that the person cares about, and the designation of a surrogate who is familiar with the person's values and can help to interpret what the person would want. If the person then wants to list what s/he would or would not want done in a given situation, the items on the list can be interpreted in light of the person's overriding values. These may include avoidance of pain, desire to be spared a lengthy period with the inability to understand or communicate, avoidance of artificial life-extending devices like respirators, or, on the contrary, the desire to struggle on with life even it means periodic or prolonged periods on a respirator.

What is important to a person may change over time. A person at age 40 may have very different views than a person at age 80. This gap in life experiences may explain why studies have shown that younger family members are likely to think that their parents don't want aggressive resuscitation or other interventions, when in fact their parents are not ready to throw in the towel and do, in fact, want aggressive interventions. Whatever the reasons, if a first advance directive is written at age 40, then the directive should probably be reviewed every ten years, and again when a debilitating illness strikes.

Filling out an advance directive can be a daunting business. Chapter Four describes some of the technical issues that often come up, and some Jewish perspectives on the process.

Paul Root Wolpe

3

FORMING NEW RELATIONSHIPS

There is a midrash that when the time had come for Aaron to
die, God could simply not bear to tell him. As a favor to God,
Moses agreed to be the one to let Aaron know that his earthly
journey was nearing its end. But Moses did not tell Aaron directly; he led him down a path of self-realization, until Aaron
finally came to the realization that he was dying by himself.
Then the two brothers began the mourning process together.[16]
Health professionals, caregivers, family members, and proxies
may well find themselves in the role Moses played for Aaron.

The recognition that one's diagnosis is terminal can be a time of profound crisis. Admitting it to oneself can be an overwhelmingly difficult task, and talking about it with loved ones is often no easier. Giving the support the dying patient needs can evoke everyone's fears about illness, pain and death. Yet the need to gather the resources of families and friends during illness, and particularly as life winds towards its end, is at the basis of the great *mitzva* of *bikur holim,* the visiting and comforting of the sick. Fortunately, illness crises often (though not always) bring family and friends to rally at the side of the sick patient (and it is later, in the chronic stages, when people are more likely to feel abandoned by loved ones). The course of the illness can include periods of shock, of loss of meaning, and of spiritual and interpersonal aloneness.

The experience of illness and dying differs greatly between people. Some people live their entire lives with chronic conditions, and the beginning of the end of life is one more stage in a long-term struggle. For others, there is an initial moment of diagnosis, or an initial event (such as a car accident, heart attack, or stroke) that signals a turning point bringing the recognition that one is entering the final phase of life. For some, the final stage of life is rapid; for others it can be drawn out for months or years. Whatever its course, the onset of terminal illness is a time to gather one's family and community, to begin, in some sense, reconnecting to what is important in life, and to initiate the long process of spiritual healing *(refuat hanefesh)* that will continue throughout the illness and the mourning that will continue after death.

In this chapter, we will look at the moments following initial diagnosis and discuss some of the ways caregivers, medical personnel, and clergy can support and comfort the terminal patient.

Refuat Hanefesh—The Healing of the Spirit

Every time we encounter another person, we establish a relationship. The relationship may be as casual as paying for a newspaper or as profound as falling in love. Terminal illness involves changing relationships; during its course, new relationships are established, existing relationships change, and old relationships are often lost. Perhaps most profoundly, people's relationships to themselves, to their bodies, and to their sense of identity are often significantly altered and reshaped as they enter the last phase of life.

When a *Mi Sheberakh* (the prayer for someone who is ill) is read during the Torah service, a *refua sh'lema,* a complete healing, is requested. The prayer goes on to define a complete healing as made up both of *refuat haguf,* healing of the body, and *refuat hanefesh,* healing of the spirit. Either can occur without the other; *refuat hanefesh* can occur even while the body is failing, just as the body can be healed without a healing of the spirit. *Refuat hanefesh* may be particularly important for those who are entering the final stages of life. People who work with the dying, and members of dying people's families, often have stories of how the dying process brought resolutions of old conflicts, a sense of well-being, and an ability to make peace with one's life and with one's spiritual connection to the Divine. *Refuat hanefesh* thus often leads to *tikun hanefesh,* the fulfillment or reintegration of the soul. Sometimes, unfortunately, *refuat hanefesh* does not begin until *refuat haguf* is no longer possible.

It is the nature of ongoing relationships, more than any other single aspect of terminal illness, that shapes the dying experience. The importance of true *rahmanut,* empathetic caring, cannot be overemphasized in the dying person's relationships with the health-care team, with caregivers, with the clergy, and with family. Though pain and fear of dying are certainly part of the struggle of terminal illness, it is loneliness, isolation, lack of information, inability to accomplish daily and life tasks, and generalized fear of the unknown that most profoundly distress the dying person. And it is relationships with others that mitigate these most difficult of problems. When the professionals and volunteers interact easily with each other and harmoniously with the patient, they form a circle of caring with great power. Those in the circle should consider which values they would like the circle to reflect.

Each of us lives within an inner biographical narrative, a story we tell ourselves about who we are, what our health is like, what our future is likely to be. We imagine a variety of possible futures, projecting forward the self we know into some imagined time years from now. Yet rarely do we project into that imagined future a chronic illness, a life-threatening accident, or the sudden onset of a terminal condition. Most of us have not rehearsed in our minds what our lives will be like as we die, and we do not usually imagine scenarios of weakness, failing health, dependency, and death.

That is why the illness encounter can be such a crisis of the self. *Refuat hanefesh* is, in part, the process of rethinking ourselves, creating a new sense of identity that includes the nature of terminal illness and the dying process, that allows us to accept, to the degree possible, the fate that we all know ultimately awaits us. *Pikuah nefesh,* usually translated as "saving a life," is one of Judaism's most sacred obligations. Yet the term literally means "the care of a soul." It is our obligation to help bring *refuat hanefesh* to those who are dying, and thereby to participate in the *mitzva* of the care of a soul.

Relationships After Diagnosis

The Talmud tells that one of Rabbi Akiva's disciples fell sick, and none of his fellow students visited him. So Rabbi Akiva went and provided solace and care to his student. "My master, you have revived me!" said the disciple, whereupon Rabbi Akiva went forth and lectured: "A person who does not visit the sick is like one who sheds blood."[17] Jewish tradition thus affirms the obligation to maintain relationships with those who are ill. The power of human connection should shape the approach of physicians, nurses, and other professionals as well as friends and family.

America tends to cast its moral stances in medicine in terms of "rights," and our biggest battles are over whether we have a right to things—a right to abortion, a right to physician-assisted suicide, and so on. But Judaism speaks little of rights and much of obligations and duties.[18] As a terminal illness progresses, caregivers should often ask themselves: what are my obligations to this person right now?

The time right after diagnosis can be scary for the patient and scary for loved ones as well. Often there is great uncertainty as to what the diagnosis really means, uncertainty that may linger virtually until the moment the person dies.

Immediately after diagnosis, however, a person usually looks to loved ones and caretakers to help interpret the meaning of the diagnosis. Common questions include "What do I do now?" and "Am I going to die?" Moments of hopefulness are interspersed with moments of despair. Medical decisions have to be made, and psychological and emotional resources have to be called in.

Different kinds of support are needed for those undergoing the trauma of terminal illness. Family members are subject to grief and confusion, yet the patient needs them to be sources of strength. Bringing both honesty and appropriate optimism under such circumstances is a huge challenge. Rabbis may be called in to give solace and guidance, and perhaps to interpret Judaism's position on medical decisions. Medical personnel are often asked to be more than conveyers of treatment and information, but appealed to as social and psychological supports. Nurses, social workers, nursing-home and hospice workers, and other health-care personnel can ease the burden of dying and establish a strong positive, personal bond with patients in their care.

The story is told that Reb Yohanan had gallstones for three and a half years, and Reb Ḥanina taught him to comfort himself by declaring, "Faithful God!" whenever he was in agony. Later, Reb Ḥanina was in pain, and Reb Yohanan asked, "Why do you not utter that incantation which you pronounced over me and which gave me relief?" Ḥanina replied, "When I was out of trouble, I could be a surety for others, but now that I am myself in trouble, do I not need someone else to be a surety for me?"[19] Times of crisis put us all in need of support and comfort, even if we usually take the role of the comforter. Sometimes the most difficult moment is seeing a person on whom others usually lean—father, mother, community leader—needing our support and comfort.

How do we give comfort and support to those we love, care for, or minister to? Certainly through *gemilut ḥasadim,* or acts of generosity and lovingkindness. Very often it is the simple things that become difficult—shopping, cleaning house, getting a ride—and it is a great *mitzva,* a community obligation, to support and care for the infirm in material ways.

However, it is not just material help we want when we are ill. As the tale of Ḥanina in the previous paragraph shows, we seek a sense of surety, of deep support from others. What we want is *raḥmanut,* or profound empathy. *Raḥmanut* is a quality that we attribute to God, one of the thirteen Divine Attributes. We ask

God to show us Divine empathy daily in our liturgy, to understand our loneliness and sense of isolation, and to embrace us in Divine love. Rabbi Leo Baeck wrote, "To place oneself in the position of our neighbor, to understand his hope and yearning, to grasp the need of his heart, is the presupposition of all neighborly love, the outcome of our knowledge of his soul."[20] Just as we ask God to bestow *raḥmanut* on us, it is one of the greatest gifts we can bestow on each other. Secular humanists may prefer a different metaphor, but for them, as well, interpersonal connection is an essential part of being human.

Making Meaning of Illness

Illness creates a crisis of meaning, and everyone who is involved with a sick person, not just chaplains, can help restore meaning to the person's world. Reactions to illness vary. Some people turn to Judaism to find that meaning, some people may turn away, and some people vacillate. Some go through a period of denial about the illness or its seriousness. Some withdraw and become depressed. Some become activists in their medical care. Some become passive and fatalistic. Some become angry with God for allowing the illness to happen, some lose faith, and some become more ritually observant or begin to attend synagogue more regularly. Others reach out to friends and family, or become more involved in their community. Any combination of these reactions is possible. Whatever the individual's reaction, everyone can benefit from ways of framing illness that provide some type of meaning.

Sensitive physicians understand that patients need to interpret illness, and don't insist that their patients adopt purely scientific explanations of illness. It is perfectly acceptable (even preferable) for a physician to decline to interpret the meaning of illness for the patient, but the sympathetic physician should allow space for the individual to struggle with the meaning of illness within a medical context.

The Shulḥan Arukh, an important code of Jewish law, states, "The Torah gave permission to the physicians to heal; hence, healing is a *mitzva*." But what is meant by "healing"? According to the Talmud, one explanation is derived from the verse in Deuteronomy (22:2): *vahashevoto lo*—"And you shall restore him to himself." To restore someone to himself or herself is not only about physical healing, obviously, but also about a full return to a state of selfhood, where the crisis in meaning attendant to illness is also resolved. The physician, according to Jewish thought, has a role in *refuat hanefesh,* healing of the spirit, just as in *refuat haguf.*

The infirm and bereaved often turn to rabbis as they struggle to make sense of illness. "Why do such things happen?" "How can God do this (to me, to my father, to my child . . .)?" People tend to look on illness as a punishment, and part of the role of the pastoral counselor is to try to reinterpret illness as part of life. While it is a mistake to try to turn suffering into a privilege and thus deny its pain and anguish, the rabbi can help the patient see illness as a natural part of life, and highlight the ways that the illness may bring family together, refocus the patient on the important things in life, and so on.

Chaplains need to listen carefully to a patient's story, which will contain clues to individuals' framing of their illness and the way they fit the narrative of their illness into their greater life narrative. Patients may find comfort in prayer, in study, or in discussion of Judaism's perspective on life, death, illness, and suffering. For those who have a religious sensibility, rituals can be comforting. Jewish rituals tend to be communal; they are intended to integrate the individual into a community. It is not unusual for those moments to be some of the most emotional for the newly diagnosed. Lighting the Shabbat candles, for example, whether surrounded by loved ones or alone, can be the precise moment when the enormity of the struggle ahead can overwhelm, or emotional stress can be released. That is a purpose of ritual, and at such moments loving support is an important reassurance that the person is not in the struggle alone.

For those who do not use Jewish ritual (and even for those who do), the presence of family itself can serve the purpose of formal ritual. Families often operate within ritualized actions of their own. Family meals often take on the form of ritual, as do going through family albums, telling anecdotes, taking walks, and so on.

Some Thoughts on Bad News

Receiving Bad News. Every time we go to the doctor with a complaint, somewhere in the back of our minds we worry about getting "bad news." While bad news is always difficult, there are ways to ease the process of informing people of bad diagnoses and to help support them through their transition.

Thirty years ago, Elisabeth Kübler-Ross, in her book *On Death and Dying,*[21] described the five stages people often experience as they begin to learn of, and cope with, a terminal illness. First comes denial, disbelief that the diagnosis could be true. Then comes anger, which can be directed at oneself, at God, and even at family members or health-care professionals. Then comes depression, as the reality of the situation sinks in and the person experiences hopelessness. Bargaining may then begin, trying to strike deals with God—give me enough time to attend my daughter's wedding, then I promise I will go quietly. Finally, in many cases, comes acceptance, as the person makes peace with illness.

Upon diagnosis, people typically undergo one or more of these stages. Often, that is the moment when others begin to assume the role of caretaker, a role that will last, for many, until the patient's death.

How do we support the newly diagnosed person who is scared and wondering about the future? Our innate tendencies to comfort may be exactly the opposite of what the person needs. We hate to see someone we know in pain, and often minimize the situation:

- "You're going to be fine!"

- "Stop being so down. You can beat this!"

- "We will take you to the best specialist in the country; we will spend anything we have to!"

These types of answers remind us of the wisdom of the Talmud, which says, "A wise one enters not into the midst of the words of his fellows and is not hasty to answer." Though such words seem comforting to the speaker, they are rarely comforting to the person with the illness. More important than promises of cures or assurances about the illness is being present and connected to the person in the moment. At initial diagnosis, individuals often feel like they have just been told their lives are over. They might as well give up now and go to bed to die. Verbal platitudes are less comforting than the knowledge that another person is there, is engaged, and is neither minimizing the illness nor promising miracle cures. Better types of responses include:

- "I will be here for you every step of the way."

- "What are you feeling now?"

- "It must be hard to get this kind of news."

- "Is this doctor one you trust? Or should we look for another you are more comfortable with?"

Elie Wiesel recounts the story of a Hasidic master who said to a student enraged at the world's evil:

> I know there are questions that remain open; I know there is a suffering so scandalous that it cannot even have a name; I know that one can find injustice in God's creation—I know all that as well as you do. Yes, there are reasons enough for a man to explode with rage. Yes, I know why you are angry. And what do I say to you? Fine. Let us be angry. Together.[23]

These types of remarks encourage and reassure, cement your concern and your involvement, and sound more real and sincere than the promises listed above.

Giving Bad News. Throughout a person's illness, he or she (and/or the family) must process an enormous amount of information. Sometimes, the decisions made on the basis of that information will have life or death consequences. It often falls to physicians, rabbis, and other caretakers to give the ill bad news.

It is important, on receiving bad news, that a person has an opportunity to express a range of emotions. The person should not be shushed, squelched or hurried. People will react differently, and their reactions and fears should be explored. Sometimes reactions will be based on inaccurate information, or may be easily transformed with a moment of time and empathy.

For physicians, delivering bad news can become routine. However common it is for the physician to give bad news, receiving bad news is almost never routine to the person getting it. Sometimes the news is devastating, and it initiates a period of profound crisis for the patient and the family. Sometimes what is perceived by the physician as bad news is not so perceived by the patient, or at least not as drastically. For some patients, such as those who have been living with symptoms and feelings that are frightening, a diagnosis may be a source of comfort, even if that diagnosis is seen by the physician as "bad." It gives the individual a sense of the reality of the problem, suggests treatments (even if purely palliative) and grounds disparate symptoms in the comfort of a label. Physicians should therefore appreciate the potential gravity of a diagnosis while allowing the patient to take the lead in framing the emotional context within which it will be received.

Often, communication between the physician and the family is more important, in terms of transmitting medical information, than communication with the patients themselves. In fact, some patients, especially elderly ones, will prefer that the details of planning and treatment be conducted with the family (see Chapter Five). While such arrangements are acceptable, it is important to determine whether it is what the patient really wants, or whether the family is trying to "protect" the patient inappropriately.

Physicians should always give bad news in person, in a setting that allows patients to bring in family members or trusted friends for support. Physicians may also want to make such support available for patients ahead of time when they know a bad prognosis is about to be delivered. Physicians should not hesitate to touch or hug patients if they perceive such touch is appropriate and can give comfort.

Truth-telling and Hope

For many years in the United States, it was assumed that people did not want to hear bad news. Doctors routinely withheld information from terminal patients, informing only their families. Such withholding is still common in many places in the world, such as Japan.

Judaism grapples with the question of how much news it is appropriate to give, and when it is permissible to shade the truth or lie. The temptation is great when the news is of devastating physical illness. Maimonides cautioned that "One must not say one thing and mean another. Inward and outward self should correspond." Yet the Talmud also understands that lying is permissible to preserve or prolong life, or for the purposes of health. David Bleich, a prominent Orthodox bioethicist, invokes the idea of *teruf hada'at,* or "troubling of the mind," to suggest that there are times when the mind must be clear and the person shielded from mental distress in order to heal fully.

However, a judgment about medical fragility should not become an excuse to shield individuals from the right to know their diagnosis and their state of health. Lying is fundamentally unacceptable in Judaism. The primacy of *emet,* truth and integrity, underlies Jewish ethics. *"Adonay Eloheykhem, emet,"* "The Divine One, your God, is truth" ends the centrally important *Shema* prayer. One must examine oneself to see whether the decision to shade the truth is being made because of the fragility and needs of the patient or because of the needs of the holder of the information.

Today, most people in the United States indicate a desire to be told the truth about their diagnosis. However, truth need not be brutal, and hope should be conveyed—not false hope, but hope appropriate to the circumstances. Hope might include the ability to extend the life span to the degree possible, to mitigate painful symptoms, or to maximize functioning.

On the other hand, doctors and other caregivers should not exaggerate hope or encourage by using false descriptions of medical breakthroughs. A physician examined Alexander Pope on his deathbed and declared his heart sounded good, his lungs clear, his pulse strong. Pope remarked, "Here I am, dying of a thousand good symptoms." People often know more through their subjective experience than even the physician can tell them, and can see through false encouragements. The dishonesty then creates alienation and distrust, making spiritual healing difficult.

Accuracy vs. Humility

People have often reported that the moments after receiving bad news are like a blank to them. Patients often misunderstand diagnosis, and either exaggerate or minimize prognosis. Family members often also express shock and can be just as inaccurate in recounting the information given to loved ones in a medical encounter.

It is important, when delivering news to be patient, to use terminology the patient can understand and to allow time for emotional response and grief. Physicians should explore what patients know and understand about the disease in question and debrief them after delivering diagnosis and prognosis to make sure they understand what the physician is trying to convey.

Perceptions of severity often differ between physicians, and so certainly can differ between the physician and the patient. There is ambiguity inherent in almost all of medicine. No one can say for certain how long a particular patient will live or predict all the implications of a particular diagnosis for any individual patient. In early sessions especially, physicians should allow patients to understand the diagnosis in their own way, as long as it is within an acceptable range of accuracy, and not insist on particular perspectives or outlooks.

Finally, the Mishnah tells us: Teach your tongue to say, "I don't know," lest you be led to lie, and be caught. Diagnosis must always be tempered by *anava,* humility, and, as the cancer surgeon Bernard Siegel has written, we must grant every patient the right to be an exception to our statistics.[24]

William Kavesh

4

END-OF-LIFE TECHNOLOGIES

Jewish tradition gives preeminence to maintaining health and preserving life. The mechanisms for bringing about these two desirable outcomes, which have varied during the long course of Jewish history, give us perspective on how religious thinking evolves.

In the Bible, Moses is described as using a special type of wood to detoxify poisonous water that the Israelites encountered in the desert.[25] The prophet Elisha mysteriously restores a young boy to life by lying down on his body—an act that some modern

Center for Jewish Ethics · Reconstructionist Rabbinical College

Jewish writers regard as the first historical record of mouth-to-mouth resuscitation.[26] The Talmud describes numerous potions, salves, and other remedies for treating a variety of medical conditions.[27] Maimonides, the most famous of many medieval rabbis who were also doctors, devotes portions of his legal code as well as separate monographs to health treatments.

Previous generations of rabbis realized that these remedies don't always work, and some became bitter at the doctors who promised more than they could deliver. Rabbi Naḥman of Bratslav, the famous Hasidic rabbi and weaver of intricate tales who lived 200 years ago (and died at age 38 of tuberculosis) is one of the most famous of these skeptics. After the doctors' failure to cure his tuberculosis with the currently available treatments, Naḥman suggested that since the Angel of Death was too busy to kill everyone himself, he appointed messengers called doctors to assist him.[28] But other rabbis respected technology, even as they greeted it with a certain skepticism. The Talmud forbade carrying amulets on Shabbat, but one that worked three times was permitted.[29]

Respect combined with healthy skepticism also typifies a reasoned approach to decision making regarding contemporary technology. New technology has made medical decision making much more complex and difficult. As noted in Chapter 2, advance directives often list several items for a person to authorize by checking off yes or no. With the advent of television medical dramas, cardiopulmonary resuscitation (CPR) has probably become the most widely known of these technologies. Its perceived power is at odds with its limited effectiveness, a situation discussed later in this chapter. Artificial breathing by use of a ventilator (breathing machine) also has achieved broad recognition and some notoriety. Many advance directives also list feeding tubes, which supply nutrition directly to the stomach or intestines when a person can no longer safely eat. Because they deal so directly with matters of life and death, these three are the most common subjects for an advance directive. They create many of the most challenging choices that patients, families and proxies face. These technologies are defined and discussed in detail later in this chapter.

There are many more technologies not discussed here for lack of space. All of them can have a profound impact on the quality of a person's life. Examples include dialysis, intravenous fluids and antibiotics, blood transfusions, major surgery, and other uncomfortable or risky interventions. Patients and families are often unaware of the reasons for these procedures or the side effects and long-term consequences that result from their use. Studies show that even when doctors attempt to explain the procedures, patients and family members often recall only a fraction of the information after they leave the doctor's office.

Although this chapter discusses cardiac resuscitation, ventilators, and feeding tubes in some detail, anyone asked to authorize use of any major intervention should inquire carefully about it before deciding. The inquiry should encompass not just the technical explanation for the intervention. The doctor should also explain the implications for the particular person considering it. For example, one might consider the value of resuscitation differently in a person with a mild stroke than in someone who can no longer communicate or someone who has recurrent pneumonias that cause considerable discomfort.

Cardiopulmonary Resuscitation

When the heart stops beating, lung function usually ceases as well. Cardiopulmonary resuscitation means restoring cardiac (heart) and pulmonary (lung) function. Some people just refer

to this as "cardiac resuscitation." This section examines the philosophical issues related to cardiopulmonary resuscitation, its technical aspects and success rates, and the Jewish values and decision-making issues involved.

Background. One of the more common things that doctors
may ask when someone is very sick is, "Do you want (or do
you want your relative) to be resuscitated?" In lay terms, what
the doctor means is, "Do you want us to try to restart your heart
and return it to beating properly if it has stopped?" This is a
rather awesome question to put to someone, since the heart
rarely starts beating properly on its own once it has stopped.
The question essentially asks, "Do you want us to accept that
death has come?" On the face of it, this seems like a peculiar
question for doctors to put to a sick patient or relative. After
all, the doctors have usually been treating the person intensively
with all kinds of treatments whose goal is to get the person
better. Up until now, no one has asked consent to stop or go
ahead with a particular treatment, unless it involved surgery or
some other risky procedure. In the case of surgery or other procedures, doctors usually ask permission to do something, rather
than *not* do something. With the exception of situations that are
clearly hopeless, the physician will automatically initiate cardiopulmonary resuscitation unless specifically instructed not to in
a document signed by the patient or a surrogate (also known as
a proxy), a person who makes decisions for the patient. The
physician will then enter a "do not resuscitate (DNR)" order
into the patient's chart.

It is not clear exactly when doctors began asking people to
decide if they wanted resuscitation. The modern practice of
CPR only started in the 1960s. Part of the impetus for asking
permission may stem from the fact that cardiopulmonary resusci-

tation has generally never been very successful. (Details about success rates are discussed below.) The concept of patient autonomy is also a late 20th-century phenomenon, as is the rise in malpractice suits related to doctors not respecting patient autonomy. Patients, usually when they are quite sick, are now asked to sign a piece of paper ostensibly to decide what previously had been relegated to God's purview: who will live and who will die. More distressing, perhaps, is that relatives or other surrogates may be asked to decide—and can spend the rest of their lives reflecting on the decision.

The heart can cease functioning for a variety of reasons. The most common cause is a heart attack, but serious infections, drug overdoses, and complications from other medical conditions can also adversely affect the heart. Resuscitation practically never works in a person who is very sick with advanced cancer or some other condition that has been getting steadily worse over a long period. The heart usually stops in that situation because the person is simply overwhelmed by the illness; the heart stopping means that the illness has, in effect, won out. There is a time to live and a time to die. God is the source of the knowledge to treat human illness, but death remains one of the great mysteries. All our technology does not hold it at bay forever.

Technical Aspects of Cardiopulmonary Resuscitation. The purpose of CPR is to restore the flow of oxygen to the lungs and to restore a normal heartbeat. To restore the flow of oxygen, the physician or another person trained in cardiopulmonary resuscitation places a special bag over the patient's mouth. The bag pushes air in and allows it to flow out, like a bellows. Mouth-to-mouth resuscitation accomplishes the same thing. In this process, some of the air is invariably forced into the stomach. This happens because the esophagus, which carries food from the throat to the stomach, is also expanded by the air flowing into the mouth. If possible, a plastic tube is inserted through the nose or mouth and directed into the upper airways of the lungs. This is called *intubation*. The bag is then connected to the tube, allowing all the air from the bag to go directly to the lungs, rather than losing some into the stomach.

While air is being pushed in by the bag, blood circulation is maintained by repeated external compression of the breastbone, located in the middle of the chest. Since the heart is located below the breastbone, each compression flattens the heart and sends blood into the arteries. When the pressure is released, the heart expands, sucking new blood into it before the next compression. Medications to stimulate the heart may also be injected. Electric shocks are often administered to the outside of the chest in an effort to restart the heart. This process is continued until the heart starts beating on its own or it becomes apparent that the process is futile.

Side Effects. Cardiopulmonary resuscitation has side effects. The most common aftermath is pain from compression of the breastbone and adjacent ribs. Older people and some chronically sick younger people often have frail bones, and rib fractures are not uncommon side effects of resuscitation attempts. Underlying organs can also be damaged. Electric shocks to the chest can leave burns—especially if a kind of regular shock is given to maintain the heartbeat for a period of time. After a period of intubation, the voice is hoarse, and it is painful to speak. While the tube is in the throat, it is impossible to talk, which can be quite frustrating. Air passed into the stomach instead of the lungs can cause painful swelling. Older patients who survive one episode of cardiac resuscitation have been known to admonish their physicians "never to do that again." External chest compression is not nearly as effective as a normal heartbeat in supplying blood and oxygen to critical areas such as the brain. Prolonged resuscitation can leave a person with irreversible brain damage, even if the heart and other organs survive.

Success Rates. How successful is cardiopulmonary resuscitation? This seems to depend on the underlying condition when resuscitation is started. At best, only about one in four people survive a cardiac arrest (when the heart stops beating or beats ineffectively). These are usually people who are healthy and have a sudden heart attack where a brief electric shock and resuscitation can restore a normal heart rhythm. Studies have shown that cardiopulmonary resuscitation invariably fails in people with widespread cancer or other advanced conditions. Studies in nursing home residents show that only about one or two of every 100 persons survives resuscitation, and they often don't survive much longer. As noted above, irreversible brain damage can occur even if the heart and other organs survive.

Survival after cardiac arrest is higher in intensive care units, but most cases of cardiac arrest are treated successfully only when patients undergoing surgery develop a cardiac arrest during the procedure. The higher success rate is probably due to the fact that the patient receiving general anesthesia for surgery is already intubated, and the heart and lung function is being monitored second by second. Therefore, the problem is recognized and treated almost instantaneously. Physicians who discuss resuscitation with patients are often put in the difficult position of trying to explain how resuscitation can succeed in some circumstances but not others. Some hospitals will not permit surgery to be done on a patient with a "do not resuscitate" instruction. Therefore, it is important in filling out an advance directive to note specifically if a "do not resuscitate" instruction would be rescinded if surgery were necessary—for example, a simple operation that would relieve severe pain.

Jewish Attitudes. From a Jewish perspective going back to the Talmud, the presence of respirations and, to a lesser extent, a heartbeat are two key signs indicating that a person is alive. In modern times, these two criteria have been supplemented by a more subtle one, evidence of brain life or death.[30] This idea also has its Jewish antecedents. Maimonides suggested that death can be said to have occurred "when the power of locomotion that is spread throughout the limbs does not originate in one center but is independently spread throughout the body."[31] A person with damage to the brain center that controls respiration can be kept alive for a long time on a ventilator. Circulation of blood to the brain and other critical organs can be maintained for a few hours with a heart-bypass machine—usually employed only during heart surgery procedures. (Artificial implantable hearts may extend this period.) Cardiopulmonary resuscitation cannot be maintained for hours. Because external cardiac compression is inefficient at maintaining adequate circulation, irreversible brain and other organ damage will invariably ensue in less than an hour. In this sense, the talmudic dictum of "no heartbeat, no life" still reflects a certain reality: with rare exceptions (children drowning in cold water, for example), inability to restore a heartbeat within 30 minutes to an hour signals irreversible damage to the heart as well as the brain and other major organs.

Making a Decision about Resuscitation. From a Jewish perspective, decision making about resuscitation involves balancing competing values. On the one hand, the principle of *pikuah nefesh* suggests that everything should be done to restore the person to life. On the other hand, it is clear that Judaism also has a long-standing aversion to interfering with inevitable processes of nature that are running their course. Thus, for example, the Shulḥan Arukh (the 16th-century code of Jewish law), contains the following instructions: "If there is anything that causes a hindrance to the departure of the soul, such as the presence near the patient's house of a knocking noise such as wood-chopping or if there is salt on the patient's tongue, and these hinder the soul's departure, then it is permissible to remove them, because there is no act involved in this at all, but only the removal of an impediment."[32] Strictly speaking, withholding resuscitation is not removing an impediment but rather refraining from an additional intervention in someone who may already be very sick. The philosophical issues involved are discussed at more length in the chapters on euthanasia (Chapter 9) and pain and suffering (Chapter 6). With regard to cardiopulmonary resuscitation in particular, it seems clear that despite Judaism's bias for life, there are circumstances in which active efforts to extend life by CPR may not be appropriate.

Advanced cancer or a persistent and irreversible coma are the two most obvious conditions in which it is appropriate to decline resuscitation. But how far should the woodchopper analogy be extended in an era of high technology? Many suggest that this perspective can be extended to other situations. One Orthodox advance directive indicates that it is reasonable to decline cardiac resuscitation in a situation where three doctors attest that a person has irreversible brain damage and an inability to recognize others or communicate, even in the absence of a terminal illness, and even if the person could live in that condition for a long time.[33] This option would allow the denial of resuscitation by someone with advanced dementia or a stroke with loss of the ability to speak or communicate, even if the condition were not immediately terminal.

What about conditions in which a person can recognize others? Certainly, in the case of cancer there is abundant medical data to indicate that resuscitation is ineffective and can be declined on the grounds that it simply is futile. But there are other conditions in which a person can recognize others, for example a person with severe and poorly controlled pain from a noncancerous condition such as severe diabetic neuropathy. Or what about the person who has severe organ failure, such as severe congestive heart failure or severe lung disease? In those situations, the person often can only walk a few feet without shortness of breath or may be short of breath at rest, may require continuous oxygen, and may be hospitalized frequently with uncomfortable tubes and blood tests.

In all of these situations, it would first be very important to determine that the person is not depressed since depression is well known to worsen a person's perception of pain and possibly other negative conditions such as shortness of breath. A psychiatrist should be engaged if there is any question about depression. Once it is clear that the person is not depressed, then the matter of pain becomes an important Jewish consideration. Judaism regards pain as a highly undesirable state (which, fortunately, is usually controllable with modern medications, though they may reduce the clarity of thinking if very high doses are required). The discomfort of shortness of breath is regarded by contemporary experts in palliative care (the care of those with a serious but incurable illness) as equivalent to pain in its level of psychological distress. A liberal Jewish perspective would regard a level of severe uncontrollable pain or shortness of breath as a legitimate reason to decline resuscitation, especially since CPR's rate of success in chronic illnesses is even lower than its success in relatively healthy individuals.

What about resuscitation in old age? Many older persons

express a desire for resuscitation, but many do not, especially those who have chronic illnesses that limit their independence or who have chronic pain. Others recall with horror the experiences of a relative or friend who underwent resuscitation only to awaken with broken ribs and brain damage. They either refuse or have their family refuse resuscitation a second time. The same talmudic source that gives 40 as the age of wisdom indicates that at age 90, one becomes stooped over and that at 100, one has a foot in the grave.[34] Senior citizens deserve aggressive treatment of illnesses, but in view of resuscitation's limited success rate and high rate of complications, family members and medical personnel should honor any request for no resuscitation by someone who feels that s/he has already lived a full life.

Ventilators

Although there have been some technical refinements over the past 50 years in the way ventilators function, the basic principles remain the same: a tube is inserted into the major airway leading to the lungs (the trachea), and air supplemented with oxygen is forced down the tube by a pump known as a ventilator (also called a respirator or breathing machine).

Background. Ventilators are used for patients whose lungs are too weak or damaged to expand enough to draw air into them and breathe out carbon dioxide. They are also necessary at times to treat conditions such as heart failure or pneumonia, where fluid accumulates in the lung tissues and blocks the flow of air. Ventilators are also used in situations where the portion of the brain controlling automatic breathing is damaged so that respiratory drive is lost.

Many people still primarily associate heart function with

life and death. Perhaps that is why the use of ventilators alone has received less notoriety than cardiopulmonary resuscitation. This seems to be the case even though adequate ventilation is critical to the success of CPR, since lack of oxygen and buildup of carbon dioxide will suppress heart function. Nonetheless, the ethical issues regarding ventilators are actually more complex than those related to CPR. As discussed above, CPR is often unsuccessful except in unusually favorable circumstances. By contrast, ventilation is usually successful in restoring the flow of oxygen to the body. CPR is maintained only for a brief period—whether or not the heart restarts. Ventilation can be maintained for years, as in the celebrated case of Karen Quinlan, which reframed the ethical issues involved by blurring the distinction between starting and stopping a ventilator if a person doesn't get better. In general circles at least, the result of the ferment was to recast the ethical issue in terms of shortening the dying process rather than terminating life. Jewish views are more nuanced, as discussed later in this chapter and in Chapter 9.

People have strong feelings about artificial ventilation. Many who have seen others on a ventilator have decided that they do not want to spend an extended period of time attached to a machine that keeps them alive but robs them of their independence. Even if they opt for resuscitation ("Give it a try" is a common answer to the awesome question), they often make it clear that if they are in such bad shape that they cannot express their wishes, artificial ventilation should only be continued for a period of days or at most a week. In an ethical sense, this use of a ventilator is viewed like any other medical intervention. It is used as a trial measure and discontinued if it does not achieve a satisfactory result. Others may experience removal of a device that keeps someone breathing as somehow an active process.

Families have much more trouble envisioning removing ventilators than do patients themselves.

Technical Aspects of Ventilators. Support of respiratory function can be accomplished indefinitely by use of a machine that automatically pushes air into the lungs through a tube. In principle, the function of a ventilator is the same as the use of the bag and tube described in the section on cardiopulmonary resuscitation, except that the ventilator replaces the person squeezing the bag. After a period of a week or two, the pressure of a tube in the lung airways can cause damage, and it is usually replaced with a tracheotomy tube, a shorter tube inserted through an incision in the lower neck. Tracheotomy tubes can be maintained or changed much more easily than tubes placed through the nose or mouth, and they are also more comfortable. As noted earlier in this chapter, it is impossible to talk while a tube is connected to a ventilator.

Side Effects. A person being treated with a ventilator who is awake enough to perceive what is happening often finds it very uncomfortable. Discomfort may occur because the ventilator has been set to deliver respirations at a certain level to maintain a proper balance of oxygen and other body gases, while the person wants to breathe faster or less deeply. This is sometimes called "fighting the respirator." In these circumstances, the physician may use medications to cause the person to relax. In unusual circumstances, the physician may even use medications to paralyze the muscles so that the respirator can do its work unopposed. This produces loss of control of all muscles in the body, which may be an upsetting experience.

Ventilators are usually disconnected from the breathing tube for short periods in order to remove secretions from the tube and to see if the person can breathe without the ventilator. When a decision is made to stop using a ventilator, the ventilator is usually not reconnected at this point.

Jewish Attitudes. There is a tradition dating back to the Talmud that life enters and exits through the nose.[35] The phrase in Genesis 7:22, "all in whose nostrils is the breath of life," was thought to provide credence for this view. The mysterious death of two of Aaron's sons was said to have been accomplished by God through the use of two intense flames of light that entered their nostrils and burned their souls. However, as we have seen above, the notion of "brain death" has supplanted this view among most Jewish thinkers of the past 20 years. This change in outlook is clearly important to a Jewish perspective on the use of ventilators. In the most severe case at least, when a person no longer has brain function, it is not necessary to initiate use of a ventilator, and there should be no compunction about removing a ventilator, because the person is no longer considered to be alive. The more complex question is what to do regarding a ventilator when a person is not brain dead.

Making a Decision about Ventilators. Jewish views on the matter of ventilators vary considerably. In parallel with its position on cardiopulmonary resuscitation described above, one Orthodox advance directive offers a person the opportunity to forego mechanical ventilation in the case of irreversible coma or inability to recognize people or communicate.[36] This is actually a more liberal approach than that of the advance directive of the Conservative movement, which restricts "do not intubate" instructions to the last six months of life.[37] In reality, most ethical issues involving intubation do not arise in settings of imminent demise—even six months may be too short. The ethical issues involve people with heart failure, ALS (Lou Gehrig's disease), chronic lung disease, strokes, and dementia. Such people may have recurrent admissions to the hospital for pneumonia or fluid accumulations in the lungs that may require a period of intubation to resolve. These people experience pain from repeated intubations, sleeplessness in an intensive care unit, needle sticks for intravenous fluids and testing, and the discomfort of being tied down in bed by all the machinery in addition to physical restraints if they become confused or agitated during the course of their treatment. Eventually many of them decide that this is not worth it and throw in the towel. From a Jewish perspective, they do not meet conservative criteria for refusing a ventilator, but there is no question that these people are in the process of dying bit by little bit with each additional hospitalization. They certainly seem to fulfill the definition of the *t'refa,* the person who is doomed to die no matter what.[38] Assuming that the person is not depressed as described above in the section on cardiopulmonary resuscitation, a liberal Jewish view would sanction the withdrawal of ventilatory support in such situations—or the use of a predetermined short trial period, beyond which the ventilator would be removed.

Feeding Tubes

Feeding tubes have become relatively commonplace as more and more people live to develop dementias, strokes, Parkinson's disease, and other neurological problems that impair swallowing. These tubes are used to supply a high-nutrient feeding that can meet all of a person's nutritional needs. Unfortunately, recent studies show that using feeding tubes does not prevent pneumonias, which has been a major reason for their use. Most people who get tubes are already very debilitated, and it is doubtful that tubes lengthen life. However, physicians and families often feel very uneasy not feeding someone when the technical capability is there, and family members feel especially uncomfortable authorizing the removal of a feeding tube if that is going to result in a relative's death.

According to American law, feeding tubes are medical technology, viewed the same way as any other medical intervention. However, many people have not adjusted their thinking to the point where they see a nutritional liquid going down a tube as different from feeding someone, even if there is little data that it helps much or substantially extends lives. What is most problematic about tubes is that they help extend, usually for a short period, lives that are already very uncomfortable and limited.

Technical Aspects. Swallowing is a complex mechanism involving the actions of the tongue, muscles of the front and back of the mouth, muscles of the throat, and finally the esophagus, the tube that carries food from the lower throat to the stomach. A key to successful swallowing is muscular coordination of all these functions, together with proper closing of a muscular cap to the windpipe, which prevents food from going into the lungs. One of the common problems interfering with swallowing is a stroke, which may interfere with the ability to move food from the front to the back of the mouth and into the esophagus. A stroke may also prevent the proper coordination of swallowing so that food may inadvertently enter the lungs and cause pneumonia.

A second common problem is an inability to swallow properly due to dementia. This problem especially affects nursing-home residents and others who have had dementia for several years. Regardless of whether the cause is Alzheimer's disease or another type of dementia, many people with advanced dementia lose the ability to perform coordinated activities. The result is the same as a swallowing problem due to a stroke. The other problem affecting people with dementia is loss of the capacity, or capability, for taking in food. Many individuals with advanced dementia will take only tiny amounts of food or liquid at a time. It may take two to three hours to feed such a person the equivalent of a single meal. A large syringe may have to be used to place liquid food into the person's mouth.

Feeding tubes are used in situations where a person is unable to swallow without allowing some of the food to enter the lungs or is unable or unwilling to take food into her/his mouth. A high-nutrition liquid, similar to liquid supplements that some people buy at the store, is put down the tube, usually by a special pump.

Feeding tubes fall into two categories: those inserted through the nose down the back of the throat and esophagus to the stomach, and those that extend through the abdominal wall directly into the stomach. The first type of feeding tube, called a *naso-gastric* tube, must be placed by the physician through the nose and throat. If the patient can cooperate, s/he is usually encouraged to swallow a small amount of water through a straw to draw the tube from the throat into the stomach. The tube does not always go down the first time. Sometimes it can inadvertently go down the windpipe into the lung. Usually, but not always, the physician is alerted to this because the patient coughs. Sometimes it is only noticed when a chest x-ray is done to see that the tube is in its proper position. Patients often find a nasogastric feeding tube uncomfortable and will yank it out if given the opportunity. Therefore, they are sometimes restrained.

The second type of feeding tube extends directly through the abdominal wall into the stomach. It is sometimes called a *PEG tube* because of the name of the procedure most commonly used to put it in: percutaneous (i.e., through the skin) endoscopic (i.e., via a lighted tube) gastrostomy (i.e., creating a hole in the stomach). At one time, these tubes were put into the stomach by a surgical procedure. Currently, they are usually placed using an endoscope, a lighted instrument about the thickness of an office-sized telephone wire that reaches from the mouth into the stomach and through which the inside of the stomach can be visualized while the feeding tube is inserted from the outside. A sedative is given intravenously during the procedure so that the person usually becomes very sleepy and is barely aware that anything is happening. Nondemented patients describe the procedure as mildly uncomfortable. Once in place, a *PEG tube* is often tolerated better than a nasogastric tube. After some time passes, most people seem to become relatively unaware of its presence.

Another approach is a *surgical jejunostomy,* in which a surgeon makes a small opening through the skin into the abdomen and directly visualizes a portion of the small bowel called the jejunum. This lies a few feet beyond the stomach. The surgeon then inserts a small tube directly into the jejunum and ties it with sutures so that it doesn't come out. The patient is usually given a mild sedative and a local painkiller to numb the skin. Some people believe that placing the tube beyond the stomach reduces the chances of pneumonia that results when feeding-tube liquid is regurgitated up the esophagus and then down into the lungs.

Effectiveness of Feeding Tubes. Even if certain feeding tubes may reduce regurgitation, many people with feeding tubes into the stomach or jejunum still develop pneumonias because they aspirate the saliva that is always being produced in our mouths. This saliva contains many bacteria that can cause serious infections. Because such people can't swallow properly, this saliva goes down the wrong way, just as food would. Studies have shown that feeding tubes don't prevent pneumonia, although they may provide some nutrition. Food supplements that are put down the tube can also cause diarrhea.

Making a Decision about Feeding Tubes. In the history of medicine, the use of feeding tubes is very recent, and Jewish perspectives still vary substantially in this area. One view is that feeding is a basic aspect of life and that we don't withhold feeding. In this argument, a feeding tube is analogous to oral feeding and therefore should be used when oral feeding is impossible or unsafe. However, Jewish tradition views eating as an act that involves placing food in the mouth and swallowing. By this reckoning, feeding through a tube is medicine.[39] That view reflects contemporary American ethical and legal decisions that feeding tubes are ethically analogous to other medical interventions, that artificial feeding is indeed artificial, and that feeding tubes can be removed the way that respirators and other technological interventions can be withdrawn.

Can these two points of view be reconciled? Certainly in premodern times, one of the most common mechanisms of dying was by ceasing the ingestion of food. Very sick people don't want to eat. Dehydration is not a painful process. It generally induces a state of lethargy and gradual decline in conscious awareness.

The notion of artificially maintaining nutrition has little in the way of Jewish historical models. Until the last century, interventions like feeding tubes simply weren't technically possible. In this respect, feeding tubes have a certain analogy to respirators, which also are modern creations. Clearly, the association of respiration and eating with life and death do have a basis in ancient Jewish traditions. The story of Elisha underscores the role of respiration in maintaining life. Regarding food, in presenting the story of Hagar and Ishmael, the Torah leaves little doubt that they would have died from dehydration if God had not intervened when they were about to run out of water.[40] Likewise, God's provision of manna to the starving Israelites in the desert underscores the simple truth that food, like breath, is a necessary condition for life.[41]

Certainly, the idea of artificially maintaining either of these two basic functions, breathing and eating, for an extended period of time is not discussed in the Torah. Yet there seems to be precedent in Jewish tradition for withdrawing respirators in certain cases, in analogy to removal of the woodchopper noted earlier. If artificial respirations in the form of a machine can be stopped, then why can't artificial feedings via a tube?

A contemporary Jewish ethicist and Conservative rabbi, Elliot Dorff, makes essentially this point, arguing that feeding tubes should be viewed as medical technology and therefore are not required treatment from a Jewish perspective.[42] Rabbi Dorff acknowledges the counterargument that food is needed by everyone, whereas medicine used to cure illness is really a foreign substance. His response is that the form of a tube feeding is more like medicine. Philosophically this may be the case, though some tube feedings certainly look like eggnog. In this respect, it may be the feeding tube itself—which must be artificially introduced, as described earlier—rather than its contents that marks the truly technological/medical aspect of the intervention.

Perhaps the comparison that works best is the analogy to the ventilator, which pumps oxygen via a tube into a person's lungs. In the same way, tube feedings are pumped into a person's stomach via a feeding tube. Breath is essential for life. When a person is no longer able to draw breath, the prognosis is hopeless and the person is suffering from great discomfort, the respirator may be viewed as an impediment to the departure of the soul from the body. Similarly, one could argue that a feeding tube is as major an impediment to the departure of the soul as the woodchopper. The ethical underpinnings of these issues are discussed further in Chapter 9.

In considering circumstances in which one might opt for not placing a feeding tube—or removing one that is simply prolonging a painful death—it is important to consider the situations in which feeding tubes are often placed. As noted above, patients with feeding tubes may have had strokes that impair their ability to swallow. Strokes significant enough to impair swallowing may also interfere with the ability to communicate and move about independently. Patients may have recurrent pneumonias requiring hospitalization, painful intravenous feedings, and blood tests. Unless the family is very motivated and wealthy enough to afford extensive home care, the person may be living in the unfamiliar environment of a nursing home. The ethical issue isn't so much about the feeding tube as about the accompanying situation that has prompted the need for the feeding tube. The overall level of discomfort, the frequency of recurrent complications, and the inevitability of decline often become the deciding factors.

Feeding tubes are also considered in cases of advanced dementia, which have similar issues. Patients with dementias advanced enough to require feeding tubes are usually quite confused. They may not recognize relatives, and they may have recurrent pneumonias requiring unpleasant hospitalizations in unfamiliar environments. Dependent on others for most of their care, they suffer from loss of control of personal functions, and often are bed-bound. The level of physical and psychological discomfort is usually significant.

Other neurological problems, such as Parkinson's disease, may also cause the patient to deteriorate enough so that normal feeding becomes impossible. Complications like those for strokes and dementia may occur.

Finally, cancer of the throat or esophagus may also physically interfere with swallowing, and a feeding tube may be necessary. In these situations, the discomfort of the cancer itself and the accompanying problems, such as skin ulcers, usually are the overriding factors affecting the person.

In all of these situations, the presence of the tube signifies the presence of a medical condition that robs the person of independence and often of the ability to communicate. The underlying condition is often the cause of significant ongoing discomfort or repeated episodes of acute illness requiring uncomfortable hospitalizations. The decision to not place a tube, or to remove (or simply stop using) a tube that is already there, is often related more to the underlying problem than to the tube itself.

Whether to authorize a feeding tube or its removal is one of the most agonizing tasks facing a relative—in some ways more distressing than authorizing removal of a ventilator. Regardless of the intellectual arguments that tube feeding is just like other technology, many family members see eggnog, not medicine, going through the tube into the person's stomach. Feeding is too basic for many people, no matter where it is going in. Many people find that the decision to remove a tube is made easier by viewing the issue from the perspective of substituted judgment—in which a surrogate tries to decide based on what s/he thinks the person would have wanted (see Chapter 5). In these situations, it seems unlikely that most people would opt for a tube as they contemplate suffering from one of the conditions that prompts placement of one.

Once a tube is removed, it is often reassuring to both families and staff (at home or in a nursing home) to try to feed the person small amounts by mouth. The person may sometimes spit the food out, but sometimes the person can take very small amounts in, even if it is inadequate to maintain nutrition or may possibly cause pneumonia. The physician can be helpful here by reassuring the family that the patient will be given pain medications if any discomfort develops once a tube is out, or if difficulty arises in breathing if a pneumonia occurs.

A Final Word About Technology and Advance Directives

Advance directives do not solve all problems, because they cannot envision all problems. Talking together as a family about advance directives is the best way to clarify as many ambiguities as possible and give caretakers a sense of what general values underlie the advance directive. Having a medically knowledgeable person, such as a doctor, participate in explaining the technical aspects, their risks and limitations, can be very helpful. Involving a rabbi or another spiritually focused person can also be very important in dealing with ephemeral but critical issues, such as the importance of extending life. This is not a task to be delegated to a clerk at a hospital, or even a lawyer, who may not understand the complex issues involved. Developing a shared understanding is hard work, but it can save a great deal of anguish later.

Paul Root Wolpe

5

FAMILIES AND TREATMENT DECISIONS

Decision Making and Familial Obligation

Throughout the course of most terminal illnesses, decisions have to be made about treatment levels and types, about the psychological and physical state of the dying person, about the appropriate location of care (hospital? nursing home? hospice?), about choosing and trusting medical teams, and about when enough is enough. When the opinions of the treatment team and the desires of the loved one are clear and the family is unified, de-

Center for Jewish Ethics · Reconstructionist Rabbinical College

cision making, however painful, may not be problematic. The problems arise when there are disputes of one kind or another, or when the dying person is incompetent to make decisions and family members with differing values are forced to make very difficult decisions for another person.

The Jewish view of such decision making is of a deep and abiding obligation. It is a great *mitzva* to assume the role of decision-maker and caretaker. In fact, it is implied in one of the Ten Commandments: *kibud av v'em,* honor your father and mother. The rabbis generalize from that commandment to an obligation to care for our families and loved ones with respect and a sense of filial obligation. The term for honoring, *kibud,* comes from the Hebrew root K–B–D, meaning heavy, weighty, or considerable. One must treat parents and all loved ones with gravity. How should one do this? What is meant by this principle of *kibud,* honoring? The Talmud explains that to express *kibud* is "to cause to eat and drink, to clothe and cover, to bring in and bring out." Duty must be manifested through behavior, through action, and not merely through an attitude of honor or an emotional attachment. *Kibud* is not an abstract concept; first, basic physical needs must be fulfilled in order for parents to be honored appropriately.

In different stages of life, the obligation "to cause to eat and drink, to clothe and cover, to bring in and bring out" can have different meanings. When the parent is still competent, the child cannot "cause" the parent to eat and drink, cannot "clothe and cover" the parent. Yet children do these things in their own way. The question, "Aren't you going to eat something, Mommy?" is the child, in her own way, causing the mother to eat, looking out for her welfare. The older child sets the table, or brings food to the table, or learns to cook. And yet, it is often at the end of life, when parents cannot do these things for themselves, that this *mitzva* is most fully and completely fulfilled.

A second obligation is the obligation for *mora,* reverential obedience to our parents. The Torah commands us both to honor and to fear our parents, the same commandment being rendered two different ways in Exodus and Leviticus. The idea of *mora* suggests that we owe our parents the respect of fulfilling their wishes, of taking seriously the desires expressed in their advance directives, or in verbal desires expressed to the DPAHC (durable power of attorney for health care) or to the family in general. These ideals of *kibud* and *mora,* while biblically mandated to children in reference to parents, are fundamentally attitudes of reverence for anyone we love who is dying, whether it is a parent, spouse, child, sibling, or friend.

Caregiving

Only recently has the medical profession begun to pay serious attention to the role of the caregiver, most often a spouse or child (though it can be a parent or even a friend). As people live longer, and as illnesses and dying stretch out over months and sometimes years, most people will spend increasing amounts of time caring for a loved one who is dying. In some ways, taking care of a loved one is the final act of devotion. As one spousal caregiver commented, "I promised to love her in sickness and in health, for better or for worse. This is the 'for worse' part. But it is just as much part of my promise as all the years that were better."

The task of caregiving is never easy. With the attention so focused on the dying family member, the toll the illness takes on the caregiver is often overlooked. Recent studies show that caregivers often become depressed, have greater rates of high blood pressure and heart disease compared to non–caregiving peers, and experience high levels of stress and anxiety. They often must interrupt their jobs and careers. Sometimes they lose their own insurance or use up precious savings. In addition, eight out of ten family caregivers are women, and many will be caregivers for years.

One important task of the caregiver is decision making. For spouses, decisions once faced as a team now often fall to the caregiver. A woman who used to split roles with her husband, for example, can suddenly find that she must now handle the family finances and home repairs, feed and clothe her infirm husband, arrange for proper care and medical attention, and do a hundred other daily tasks alone. In addition, she may now have to make serious medical decisions for her husband, the kind of serious decisions that she was used to making as a couple. In cases of children now caring for their parents, traditional roles are reversed, and the children may be making important decisions for the very people they have always turned to for advice about their own decisions. In addition, the physical, psychological, financial, and emotional toll of caregiving can be overwhelming.

That is why the obligations of *kibud* and *mora* discussed above are not absolute. Maimonides ("Rambam") writes that those whose fathers or mothers become deranged should try to provide care for them in a manner appropriate to their mental state until they "receive mercy" (that is, until they heal or die). But if the child cannot bear this because of the parent's excessive derangement, the child should withdraw and arrange for others to treat the parent in an appropriate manner. In other words, we have an obligation to those we love to care for them and to stand by them. But Rambam understands that there can come a point when care for a loved one becomes self-destructive, or conflict-laden, or in other ways so compromises the caretaker's ability to show respect and honor for the parents, that it is better to relinquish the caretaker role to others. However, that does not mean one may abandon a parent; it means the child finds a competent caretaker to assume the obligations of feeding, clothing, and caring for the parent in the child's place.

Sometimes, the most difficult part of caregiving is the loss of community. As caregivers reduce community activities to cater to their loved ones' needs, friends often drop away, causing an increasing spiral of isolation and loneliness. At just the time that caregivers need support to make serious decisions about their loved ones' care, they may feel abandoned. Yet caregivers need not make serious medical decisions alone. In addition to the family, other support is available to caregivers. Synagogues, hospitals, nursing homes, and hospice programs can often connect caregivers to support groups or networks of others struggling with the same issues.

It is incumbent upon the community to reach out not only to the infirm, but to caregivers as well. Synagogues are their members' Jewish communities, so they have an obligation to support those with illness in their families. We should not think of *bikur holim,* the obligation of visiting the sick, as limited to the individual with an illness. Family units experience illness together. Couples are sick when either partner is unwell, and we are all accountable for *tza'ar ba'aley hayim,* reducing suffering, including the suffering of the caregiver.

Decision Making and Jewish Tradition

While Jews have traditionally looked to *halakha* to help with these challenging questions, decision making is an equally difficult process in rabbinic literature. Even in the Talmud it is often the source of argument and disagreement. The Talmud does not go into medical issues in particular depth or breadth, and many contemporary questions have only the faintest connection to cases in the text. The *halakha* therefore offers some guidance for the difficult decisions to be made at the end of life, but the complexity of modern medical decision making calls on us to use Jewish principles in new ways, to elaborate and generalize the kinds of ideas derived from our long tradition to novel situations that evoke novel ethical dilemmas. Since the *halakha* is not decisive for most Jews, liberals use its insights but, for many types of decisions, move them from legally based arguments to values-based ones.

For example, it is a halakhic principle that someone whose life is in danger can be compelled to take medical treatment, even against his or her will. One must accept treatment if it will improve one's condition, unless that treatment is itself hazardous. Nonetheless, the rabbis were often very flexible about how they understood the term "hazardous." It may be hazardous to force people to accept treatments that they are unwilling to undergo, for example.

The idea of mandatory treatment is balanced by the category of the *goses,* someone who is in the process of dying and who need not be disturbed with treatments. However, there is much dispute today about when a person might be a *goses,* and what such a term even means when the dying process can be so altered by respirators, artificial nutrition and hydration, and other technologies. Liberal Judaism has broadened traditional halakhic principles, added values–driven methodology, and leavened them with the modern historical experience of our people. American law allows the patient (or proxy) to refuse treatment at any time, and grants individuals control over their bodies as a fundamental human right. A perfectly healthy person, who could benefit by treatment and perhaps even be saved by it, may refuse such treatment. However, for Jews looking to Jewish tradition for guidance, such a perspective must be tempered. Judaism sees life as a rare and precious gift, and the continuance of life as a profound obligation. From the Jewish perspective, refusal of treatment should have a justification that merits the risking of life.

Finally, even within an appreciation of the sacredness of life, the difficult issue is determining when treatment will have no lasting effect on the preservation of life, when our moral obligation shifts from preservation to attending to the dying process in order to make it as comfortable and easy as possible. The transition from aggressive treatment, or treatment in general, to a state of palliative treatment, is a difficult one for any family to make. By that time, the dying person is often only marginally part of the decision-making process, and the family must step in to make difficult decisions that will clearly lead to their loved one's death. The fact that the loved one is already dying does little to alleviate the emotional pain of making such a decision in all its finality. This is certainly the time when a family should come together as a unit and be mutually supportive. Friends, the medical-care team, and the rabbi all can have a profoundly important role to play in this process.

In medical decision making, each person has a role. If the dying person is competent to make decisions, then his or her decisions about the nature of care must be respected in order to preserve *kavod,* dignity, and autonomy. Even when the dying person makes decisions that are contrary to the desires of the caregiver or family, they must respect the individual's right to self-control. Of course, patients who are dying or who are in pain often become desperate and ask their loved ones to engage in desperate measures, and we have no obligation *ourselves* to engage in behaviors we feel are immoral or wrong, even for the benefit of the dying.

Decision-Making Capacity

Medical decisions must be made from the moment of diagnosis of a terminal illness through the moment of death. Along the way, the dying person, who may have started out fully able to make decisions, can lose some or all capacity to make healthcare decisions. It is important to remember that the capacity to make such decisions is not an all-or-nothing proposition. People may be fully able to make certain kinds of decisions (such as when they need pain medication) and yet not be aware or lucid enough to make other kinds of decisions (such as whether to undergo major surgery). Unfortunately, legally a person is either generally "competent" or "incompetent," and medical teams often adopt the same language. A much better concept is the idea of "capacity," which suggests a range of abilities. People should be given full right to make judgments about issues that are within their capacity to judge. Making this a reality is a task for the person who bears the decision-making proxy.

The time often comes when a family must take over the medical decision making for their loved one. It helps if the person has written an advance directive, and if there is a single family member or friend who has been designated the decision-maker through durable power of attorney in health care (DPAHC). Yet even with such protections, the process can be difficult and contentious within the family and between the family and the medical team.

Surrogate Decision Making

A basic assumption, in both American society and in much of Jewish writing, is that family members are best able to make decisions for people who have lost the capacity to make judgments for themselves. Families, presumably, know the person best, can anticipate what he or she would have wanted, and can make decisions with the person's best interests at heart. Families have usually maintained a long-term intimate contact with the individual. Another less commonly noted advantage of family decision making is its collaborative nature. Concerned family members, who have personal knowledge of the individual, can talk about what the person might have wanted, bringing in the person's values, the family's values, and a shared family culture and history.

Of course, this is an ideal view. Some families are estranged from particular members, and may not be in the best position to make informed decisions about what that person would want. Even in intact families, there is often conflict, either about what the person would have wanted, or what is in that person's best interest. Note that these are two separate ideas:

- Substituted judgment is making decisions for an incompetent patient according to what *that person* would choose to do if competent.

- Best-interests decision making is making decisions for an incompetent person according to *what the decision-maker* thinks is in that person's best interest. (For example, we tend to use a best-interests standard with children.)

Modern bioethics strongly advocates using a substituted-judgment standard whenever possible, so that we can maximize individuals' rights to be treated as they would have wanted to be treated. There are times, however, when decision-makers do not know what the now-incompetent person might have wanted in a particular situation, so they must do what they believe to be in the person's best interest.

Sometimes, what is perceived to be in the patients' best interest and what the patients themselves would do if they could make the decision are not the same thing. Conflicts may arise when the family takes over the decision making of an individual who has ideas or values that are at odds with those of other family members. Does the family use substituted judgment and decide based on what "father would want us to do," even if the family does not share those values, or should the family not try to do what they think father might have wanted but instead focus on "what's best for father?" Similarly, family members will often differ about what exactly father would have wanted had he been able to make the decision for himself.

The struggle highlights why it is so important, before we get sick, to choose someone who shares our values as durable power of attorney for health care (see Chapter 2). A DPAHC will be able to make less stressful and more reliable decisions if he or she shares the beliefs and values of the individual. In the absence of a designated DPAHC, decisions should be made, to the degree possible, as substituted judgments rather than best interests. We owe our loved ones the respect of asking what they would have wanted in that situation, no matter how our values might differ. This is a question of *kavod*. To the degree that the patient is aware of what is happening, following the individual's desires will have a positive impact on the potential for *refuat hanefesh*, healing of the spirit.

Supporting Decision Making

Decision making often doesn't go easily. Families may disagree about diagnosis or prognosis; some family members may not trust the doctor; family members may ally with different health-care professionals working on the same case who have slightly different views of what's going on; families may believe that there are further choices that have not been presented to them; families that have taken care of a dying person for a very long time may be emotionally burned out, physically exhausted, and financially depleted; families may see little in front of them, if their loved one lives, except months or perhaps years of care-taking. Yet families usually also recognize the obligation to assume the responsibility of making decisions for loved ones at the end of life.

Emotions often complicate decision making. Grief can cloud judgment, make people unrealistically optimistic, or push people to hold on when it might be better to let go. Grief can also emerge as conflict; grieving family members, having difficulty confronting their grief directly, can release it as anger, hostility, or blame on other family members. Another common emotion is guilt—that not enough has been done, that fights or conflicts with the loved one have not been resolved, that one member of the family has been estranged or has not participated "enough" in a loved one's care. When decisions over care must be made, this is not the appropriate time for such dynamics to cloud the issue, but when do family conflicts ever emerge at the "appropriate" time?

In medical decision making, often the decision is treated as if one answer should be "right" in some absolute sense. Rarely is the choice so black and white. When differing opinions are expressed, other parties, including the physician, the rabbi, and the social worker can be of great help in informing the family of accepted practices, in suggesting actions, and in facilitating family decision making.

The Rabbi. The physician, the rabbi, and the patient, including the family, make a triad of decision-makers in contemporary

Jewish thought. Just as the best physicians are concerned not only with healing the body, but with healing the mind and spirit as well, so the rabbi should be concerned with healing the body as well as the mind and spirit. The rabbi is concerned not only with the decisions that patients and their families make, but with the processes and intentions behind those decisions. The rabbi can be a guide and a confidant in those kinds of decisions.

However, the rabbi's role is also to act as the interpreter of Jewish ethics, and of the role that Jewish tradition can play in the healing process. In contemporary liberal Jewish thought, the rabbi serves not as a final authority dictating permissible and impermissible behavior, but as a learned and experienced guide to Jewish tradition. The rabbi phrases questions and answers inquiries in ways that provide guideposts to suffering individuals and their families as they negotiate their way through the difficult series of decisions that confront any family in the dying process. The rabbi can also serve as an interpreter or go-between, helping the patient describe and justify medical decisions to the health-care team. Equally, the rabbi can serve in the opposite capacity, interpreting and translating the concerns and recommendations of the physician for the family. Rabbis well-trained in hospital chaplaincy may be better able to serve the role of interpreter of complex medical ideas, but any rabbi can also serve in a pastoral care role, less as an interpreter of technical medical knowledge than as a facilitator who can recognize the stresses, conflicts, and difficulties of the medical decision-making role.

How the health-care team deals with the rabbi's role may depend on the physician's religion or the religion of other members of the health-care team, as well as the type of hospital or facility in which the decisions are being made. Catholic and Jewish hospitals often—but by no means always—display greater sensitivity to religious needs. Nursing homes tend to be sensitive to the religious needs of their residents, and hospice is generally extremely sensitive to these kinds of issues. For those institutions where religious needs are not given extensive support, the rabbi can be invaluable as a go-between when decision making becomes difficult, or when the decisions of families are in conflict with the recommendations of their physicians or institutions. For families with advance directives, especially insofar as those advance directives are prepared from within the Jewish tradition, the rabbi's advocacy for the decisions made by the patient and family can be particularly persuasive.

The Physician. Other professionals also have a role to play in medical decision making. The first, of course, is the physician. A beautiful midrash describes the importance of the physician's role, and also its nature:

> If one does not fertilize and plow, the trees will not produce fruit. If the fruit is produced but is not watered or fertilized, it will not live but die. So too with regard to the body. Drugs and medications are fertilizers, and the physician is the tiller of the soil.[43]

The expectations from Jewish tradition are that physicians will do everything in their power to prolong life, when appropriate, but will avoid measures that prolong dying. The physician, however, suffers from the same dilemma as the family. How do we know when that transition has been made? There is no magical physical moment when living gives way to dying; our lives are seamless journeys from birth to death, and divisions are our attempts to make sense of that journey.

We turn with trust to physicians for their experience with dying, their understanding of the disease course, their prognosis for the future, their understanding of options. We take the advice of physicians seriously; that is why patients so often decide to do what the doctor recommends. But often the decision to be made is not one of medical judgment, but of values. In those situations, the physician is just another voice in the process of considering the appropriate action. Increasingly physicians accept that and support family decision making by contributing advice and letting the family work their way to their own solutions.

Decision Making and Sh'lom Bayit

While often difficult and painful, the process of attending a loved one who is dying can provide families with a time of coming together. Shared decision making creates opportunities to rediscover bonds of love and to put aside differences for the sake of the loved one. Some families, on the other hand, have little experience making shared decisions. They may feel estranged, may have conflicts over values or religious observance, or may tend to make even small decisions through argument and annoyance rather than collaboration and compromise.

In one common scenario, for example, a family member has been acting as primary caregiver, while other family members, perhaps because they live further away, have had less contact with the loved one. When crucial decisions need to be made, the more distant member may feel an equal right to make decisions, may even feel the need to assuage guilt by rushing in to "save" the loved one. The caretaker member, on the other hand, feels better equipped to make decisions, and may resent the participation of the more distant relative. The primary caregiver may also be more willing to let go of the loved one, as the intimate contact has allowed a more intimate knowledge of the patient's suffering and a sense of personal closure.

These tensions are difficult to understand and defuse if they only arise at the end of life when crucial decisions must be made. Family members should engage in shared decision making early in the process and learn to negotiate and compromise early. It is helpful if the primary caregiver and other family members communicate early and often so that they approach the latter stages of the process with greater mutual understanding.

The Jewish value of *sh'lom bayit,* keeping peace in the family, becomes even more important at such stressful times. Contentious families should use the opportunity to show forgiveness and to let go of being "right" in the service of everyone's dignity. Often, starting a discussion with a prayer can set the right tone of humility and service that can lead to a deeper place of family togetherness.

Sheila Segal

6

PAIN AND SUFFERING

Carol, a 58-year-old psychologist, wife, and mother of three grown sons, was suffering from cancer that began in her jaw and spread to her tongue and throat. She had undergone multiple surgeries and intensive doses of chemotherapy and radiation. After four years of recurrences, treatments, and complications, Carol was frail and unable to speak above a whisper, but she maintained her clients and relished the time she spent with her family. Eventually Carol was hospitalized because the cancer in her throat was making it difficult for her to breathe or swallow.

Center for Jewish Ethics · Reconstructionist Rabbinical College

She sat with her husband Dave as her doctor explained that she would soon need a ventilator to enable her to breathe. Since there wasn't enough room to place a tube down her throat, a surgical tracheotomy would be required. What's more, since she would be unable to swallow food or drink, she would need to have a feeding tube inserted directly into her stomach for nutrition. Any further treatment of the cancer itself would have to be suspended.

That night Dave lay in bed thinking about all the pain his wife had already endured, and he asked himself how much more anyone could expect of her. How could she accept a breathing machine and a feeding tube when they would cause so much more suffering, without any hope of improvement? But if she didn't agree to these measures, would she have to endure a horrible, gasping death? Dave was swimming in a sea of fear and confusion. He didn't know how they could ever make such a terrible decision.

How do people make "terrible decisions" like the one presented to Carol and Dave? Most people cannot imagine it, but the questions that Dave asked that night raise ethical issues that most of us will face at some point in our lives, in relation to ourselves or someone close to us. As medicine continues to make advances in extending lives, more questions will arise about the benefits of treatment in light of the pain and suffering involved, and about the availability of pain medication and the ethics of pain management. The experience of pain and suffering is at the heart of medical decision making at the end of life; this chapter will offer Jewish principles and values to guide the decision-maker through the ethical dilemmas that arise from the experience and treatment of pain.

Why Is This Happening?

From the beginnings of Judaism to our own times, Jews have struggled to understand pain and suffering. According to several passages in the Bible, disease and illness are punishments for sin, but the Bible offers no satisfactory explanation for the suffering of those who are righteous. The book of Job certainly suggests that people do not necessarily do anything to warrant what happens to them. Job suffered through no fault of his own. In response to this apparent injustice, some of the rabbis of the Talmud suggested that God gives good people "opportunities" to suffer in this world so that their reward will be even greater in the world to come. To other sages, this concept, known as "sufferings of love," offers no solace. In a famous talmudic story, one great rabbi sits by the sickbed of another, and both admit that their "sufferings of love" are not welcome to them, either in this world or in the world to come.[44]

Maimonides, the medieval rabbi and physician, placed the problem in a broader context. From his perspective as a philosopher and a scientist, he explained that pain and suffering are inevitable parts of human experience, caused by nature's randomness and the world's lingering imperfections. Thus every form of life is susceptible to injury, disease, decay, and eventually death. But why some people are afflicted more than others is a question that human beings cannot answer. Such knowledge, Maimonides states, exists only in the mind of God.[45]

Degenerative diseases, fatal illnesses, crippling accidents, untimely deaths—all these afflict good people as well as bad. And when they happen to us, we may turn to God and ask, "Why me?" Rabbi Harold Kushner rejects the tendency to believe that the pain and suffering we experience must be "God's will," or that "God doesn't give us more than we can bear." In his modern classic *When Bad Things Happen to Good People,* Kushner asserts that the "bad things" that happen should not be interpreted as divine decrees, moral judgments, or tests of faith. Everything that happens to us, he believes, is not necessarily the will of God, and the belief that God wants us to suffer—that we deserve to suffer—can unnecessarily make the pain even harder to bear.

For Kushner, as for other liberal Jewish theologians, the question to ask is not, "Why is God doing this to me?" but "How can God help me to bear the pain?" This view of God as a source of comfort and strength and a healer of the spirit appears in many Jewish sources, from the Bible to contemporary theology. It is especially evident in the book of Psalms, where God is the Compassionate One who is "near to all who call sincerely" (Ps. 145), who is with us as we "walk through the valley of the shadow of death" (Ps. 23), who "binds our wounds and heals our broken hearts" (Ps. 147). Jewish liturgy is filled with images of a God who raises us, heals us, and frees us.[46]

Dr. Dan Gottlieb, a noted psychologist who became paraplegic at the age of 33 as the result of an automobile accident, has described the spiritual healing that may come with the awareness that God is near to us in our suffering. In the midst of his excruciating pain and profound despair, Gottlieb came to the realization that, in return for faith, God promises one thing: companionship. For Gottlieb, God's companionship made it possible to go on.[47] For some people the experience of pain may result in a new or heightened awareness of God's presence, perhaps even a feeling of being closer to God than ever before. But it is important to remember that in Judaism, pain is never sought or valued as an end in itself, even as a way of seeking atonement or experiencing holiness, *kedusha.* Rabbi Elliot Dorff stresses this point, arriving at the conclusion that "Since pain is not a way to obtain holiness [in Judaism], it is our duty to relieve it."[48]

Pain Must Be Relieved

The duty to relieve pain, Rabbi Dorff explains, is thus an aspect of the obligation to heal others and to seek healing for ourselves. It reflects the Jewish view that our bodies are entrusted to us by God and, as long as we live on this earth, it is our sacred duty to be *shomrey haguf,* guardians of our bodies. The Talmud even states that it is forbidden to live in a city without a physician.[49] Thus Judaism instills the value of preserving health, as well as the value of healing the spirit and the body, *refuat hanefesh urefuat haguf.* If we cannot bring healing by curing the disease, we must at least try to do so by relieving the pain.

Judaism recognizes that relief of pain is not solely the province of medical science since pain afflicts the *nefesh* (spirit) as well as the *guf* (body). The extent of a person's suffering depends on many factors that are not even strictly medical. Often physical pain is intensified by the fear that it will be unrelieved or become even worse. Or it may be felt more intensely if the patient is also experiencing some spiritual malaise or emotional distress. Recent losses, unresolved guilt, troubled personal relationships, or simple loneliness can make an individual more vulnerable to physical pain and more desperate for pain medication.

Studies have shown that patients whose emotional and spiritual needs are addressed actually require less medication for pain. Therefore, when making medical decisions at the end of life, whether for ourselves or for others, it is important to consider what non-medical factors may be contributing to the experience of pain and suffering. Chaplains are trained to make this type of spiritual assessment, and they can help everyone to better meet the patient's spiritual needs. From a Jewish perspective, family and friends, as well as the patient herself, all have an essential role to play in the effort to relieve pain.

The importance of companionship to those who are suffering pain is recognized by the earliest Jewish sources. A midrash on the book of Genesis relates that the Holy One actually came to visit and comfort Abraham after his circumcision. And so all Jews—no matter how important or busy—are expected to emulate God's example by engaging in the sacred activity of *bikur holim,* visiting the sick. According to the Talmud, the impact of a visit is measurable, for each visitor "takes away 1/60 of the pain."[50] Conversely, failing to visit someone who is ill is like "shedding blood," a clear violation of the commandment, "Do not stand idly by the blood of your neighbor."[51] Thus the simple act of *bikur holim,* of visiting someone who is sick, is elevated to the level of *pikuah nefesh,* the imperative to do whatever is needed in order to save a life.

Patients in hospitals and nursing homes attest that the caring presence of others does help them to endure their pain. A person who is preoccupied with pain can be soothed and revived by another human being—family, friend, physician, or clergy—who approaches her in a spirit of *hesed* and *kavod,* lovingkindness and respect. Offers of heartfelt concern, a hand to squeeze, a warm blanket, a favorite food, or even a sip of water—examples of what Judaism calls *gemilut hasadim,* deeds of lovingkindness—actually have the power, as the Talmud says, to "take away some of the pain."

A hospital chaplain followed the sounds of sobbing to a room where a young woman with AIDS lay pleading for her pain medication, but as the chaplain held her hand, prayed and talked with her, the woman seemed to forget her pain and eventually drifted off to sleep. When a nursing home volunteer offered to get a nurse for the resident who was howling, "Help me, I'm in pain," the old woman explained that the pain was not in her body but in her *neshama,* her soul; with another human being attending to her *neshama,* the woman's wailing subsided completely. In both cases the pain was relieved through expressions of *raḥmanut,* compassion, for the suffering of another.

It isn't easy to be with someone who is very ill, especially when the person is in pain. Often we try to avoid the subject, but allowing those who are ill to talk about their pain can provide real relief. In addition to asking how they are feeling, what's on their minds, and what they need, Judaism guides us to relate to the individual person, and not the illness. Visitors who bring up topics of previously shared interest help dying individuals hold on to who they are even as their lives may be coming to an end. For someone who is at the end of life, it is wonderful to encourage reminiscences of the people, events, and accomplishments that have been especially meaningful. The renewed sense of meaning engendered by "life review," a directed process of remembering, can be a powerful antidote to the physical and emotional pain of dying.

Another important element in the Jewish approach to relieving pain is *tefila,* prayer. Traditionally, *bikur ḥolim* includes a prayer by the visitor that God will be merciful to the one who is sick. *Ḥolim,* those who are sick, also find it comforting to know that their names will be included in the traditional *Mi Sheberakh* prayer for healing during synagogue services. Whether prayers are offered at the bedside or in the synagogue, it feels good to know that one is being prayed for.

Praying for oneself, or "talking to God," is also good therapy for pain. Many of our traditional prayers, especially the Psalms, give us the language we need to bring our pain and despair before God. Rabbi Naḥman of Bratslov, the popular Hasidic teacher, also encouraged talking to God in our own words, "as you would talk to your very best friend." Emphasizing the accessibility and fluidity of prayer, he urged: "Express your innermost thoughts and feelings before God each day in the language you are most familiar with. . . . Even if all you can say to God is 'Help!' it is still very good."[52] During times of suffering, even those who have little previous experience with prayer may find comfort in traditional *tefila,* or in spontaneous personal prayer.

Even if words of prayer do not change the medical situation, prayer can alleviate pain by promoting feelings of peace and hope, as well as a renewed sense of God's presence. *Nigunim,* the wordless melodies of prayer, can be particularly therapeutic, tapping memories and emotions that are difficult to describe, sometimes even lifting the spirit into moments of transcendence. For one who is not especially religious, other types of music— jazz, opera, classical—can open the heart and free the spirit, having the same soothing and cathartic effect as prayer. The important thing is to determine what is truly "soul music" for a particular individual.

Visits to the bedside, *bikur holim,* and prayers for the sick, *tefila,* have long been our primary Jewish resources for relieving pain and sustaining life, and they remain so today. Whether or not an individual has the benefits of companionship and/or prayer will affect the experience and assessment of pain as well as the medical treatment that is required.

Conflicting Values

Just as physical pain usually cannot be treated without addressing emotional and spiritual needs, the obligation to relieve pain cannot be separated from other Jewish values and duties, such as: *b'tzelem Elohim,* the belief that human beings are created in the divine image; *pikuah nefesh,* the duty to save a life that is imperiled; and *lo tirtzah,* the prohibition against murder. Sometimes medical decisions that arise at the end of life seem to bring these values into conflict. It is especially complicated when the goal of relieving pain is enmeshed in decisions involving feeding tubes, ventilators, dialysis, or amputation. What if the rejection or discontinuation of a painful treatment results in a patient's death? What if the amount of morphine required to relieve pain also diminishes the patient's ability to breathe and hastens death?

These are examples of the ethical dilemmas that frequently arise as we make end-of-life decisions for ourselves and others. It helps, of course, if each of us has an advance directive stating our values and our treatment preferences, but applying these guidelines to actual decisions is not always a clear-cut matter. Whatever the situation, Judaism teaches us to approach these decisions in a spirit of *yirat Shamayim,* awe and humility before the Holy One; with reverence for the *tzelem Elohim,* the divine aspect of every person; and with a commitment to doing what is *letovato,* in the best interest of the individual who is ill. The concept of *letovato* suggests that sometimes acting in the patient's best interest means doing whatever is necessary to preserve life, but sometimes it means relieving pain and allowing the natural process of dying to proceed.[53] Sometimes the sanctity of life is violated by prolonged suffering without hope of recovery, and sometimes it is affirmed by acceptance of *eyt lamut,* the reality that for each of us there is, inevitably, a time to die.

Definitions of "Dying"

Many of the pain-related decisions made by patients, their families, and their physicians depend on whether or not a person is actually at the end of life, but making that determination is much more complicated than it used to be. For centuries rabbinic authorities have used the term *goses*[54] to designate an individual who is actively dying and is not expected to live more than 72 hours.

A person in this state should not be disturbed in any way that would cause more pain or interfere with the process of dying, but it is permissible to withhold or withdraw medications and machines that prolong the process. At the same time, the obligation to relieve pain means that one should do what is necessary to make a *goses* comfortable, even if there is a possibility of hastening death.

Another relevant rabbinic term is *t'refa*,[55] literally "an imperiled life." This is a broader category that describes people who are gravely ill but do not meet the specific conditions for being a *goses,* namely, being within 72 hours of death. However, in the world of contemporary medicine, with so many medications and machines available to help extend the lives of those who are mortally ill, the categories of *goses* and *t'refa* have been blurred. A person whose breath is as weak as a flickering candle can now live for weeks, even months, on a ventilator. A person whose kidneys no longer function can be kept alive by dialysis machines that do the work of these vital organs. A frail elderly person whose body no longer craves or ingests food can have a feeding tube inserted that provides nourishment for months. Situations like these have led Jewish medical ethicists to be more flexible about the time frame attached to the *goses* and extend permission to withhold or withdraw life support to the *t'refa* as well.[56]

Whether or not we feel bound by the precepts of Jewish law, the terms *goses* and *t'refa* help us understand the Jewish view that there are stages in the process of dying. With the boundaries of these stages now blurred, making it more difficult to say when a person is actively dying, liberal Jewish ethicists would consider a person to be at the "end of life" if he or she is suffering from a disease or condition for which there is no cure and no reasonable hope of improvement. If the person is also in pain, the following ethical principles may serve as guidelines for the terrible decisions we have to face.

1   When a person is dying, and especially if the person is in pain, any intervention that prolongs the dying process may be rejected or discontinued.

2   When there is no reasonable hope of a medical cure, treatment that causes or prolongs pain may be rejected or discontinued.

3   There are situations in which acceptance of death is in the best interest of the individual.

4   When there is no reasonable hope of a cure, pain must be treated as aggressively as necessary.

The situations described below show us how these principles may be applied.

Removal of Impediments to Dying

Sharon, a vibrant wife, mother, and teacher, was 46 years old when her annual mammogram revealed a malignancy. Immediately she began two months of chemotherapy, followed by a mastectomy and six more months of chemotherapy. Because the cancer had spread to her lymph nodes, she underwent a stem-cell transplant as well, a treatment she described as a horror. A year after her initial diagnosis, Sharon was ready for reconstructive surgery and a subsequent return to work, but tests revealed a large tumor in her brain stem. Putting everything else on hold again, she immediately went into surgery for removal of the tumor, but after two weeks of follow-up radiation treatments, doctors discovered still more cancer in her brain. With chemotherapy and radiation no longer an option, they suggested a new type of laser treatment to attack the spreading tumors. Sharon was ready for anything. She said she would even undergo another stem-cell transplant if it might help. That's how much she wanted to live!

While Sharon was still recovering from the surgery, she contracted a bacterial pneumonia that was resistant to antibiotics. Her breathing became painful, and she frequently gasped for more air. Doctors tried to save her lungs by putting her on a breathing machine, a ventilator, but there was no significant improvement. Sharon, ever the optimist, would give her family a valiant "thumbs-up" sign, but she was often sedated to keep her from grabbing at the breathing tube and the intravenous lines. After two weeks the doctors told her husband and daughter that the time limit for intubation was approaching, and a choice would have to be made between performing a tracheotomy to sustain her airway or removing the ventilator altogether. Either way, they offered no hope of recovery from the disease. If the ventilator were removed, doctors assured them, Sharon would receive enough medication and oxygen to keep her calm and comfortable until she died.

In a 16th-century legal commentary, Rabbi Moses Isserles wrote: "If there is anything that causes a hindrance to the departure of the soul, such as the presence near the patient's house of woodchopping or salt on the patient's tongue, then it is permissible to remove them, because there is no act involved in this at all but only the removal of an obstacle to dying."[57] If one should be sensitive to the noise of woodchopping or to salt on the tongue as obstacles to the soul's departure, then how much more of an obstacle is a machine that breathes for a person whose lungs are destroyed?

No family could have been more devastated than Sharon's,

but it became clear to them that keeping her on a ventilator was prolonging her suffering without any hope of recovery. They had watched her gasping for oxygen, gagging on the breathing tube, and tossing about in pain. They saw her grabbing for the tubes and the IV lines as if trying to break free. With her lungs ravaged by disease and the cancer still spreading in her brain, Sharon's family concluded that it was in her best interest, *letovata,* to "allow her soul to depart." To make her as comfortable as possible while she was dying, they had her moved to a hospice facility. There they could be with her around the clock, surrounding her with their love until the moment of her death.

Rejection of Treatment That Prolongs Pain

Ethel, age 72, did not sleep during her dialysis treatments, but she kept her eyes closed as if shutting out the horror. When she opened her eyes, they were full of sadness and fear. Ethel was new to dialysis, the treatment that removes, purifies, and recycles all the body's blood when the kidneys can no longer perform this vital function. After many years of diabetes and related complications, her kidneys functioned so poorly that she needed these treatments in order to stay alive.

It took two months of hospitalization and rehabilitation for Ethel's body to adjust to dialysis. She was then able to go home with her daughter. But five weeks later she was hospitalized again to replace the dialysis shunt, and in another two months she was back for treatment of an irregular heartbeat and an infected foot that would not heal. Ethel was extremely discouraged. She described her life as intolerably constricted and without pleasure. She had chronic pain in her legs, was unable to walk, and no longer went out of the house—except for her three weekly trips by ambulance to receive dialysis. Though the treatments kept her alive, she hated every minute of them. What's more, they did not seem to help her feel any better on the days in between. She felt that the quality of her life was steadily declining.

A month later Ethel was back in the hospital, this time with a blood clot in her left leg, and her doctors recommended a surgical procedure to restore the flow of blood. They also looked again at the infection on her right foot, which was growing worse, and recommended partial foot amputation to prevent it from spreading up her leg. At that point Ethel said, "Enough." She told her children that she couldn't take any more, that her life was just too painful for her to go on. With their support, she not only rejected the proposals for surgery, but terminated her dialysis treatments as well. Pain medications, given at home under hospice care, helped Ethel through the week that passed until her death.

A haunting early rabbinic tale, a midrash, tells of a very old woman who came to her rabbi and expressed feelings similar to Ethel's. The woman complained that her life had lost all meaning and pleasure, becoming so hideous that she wished to depart from the world. The rabbi responded by asking the woman how she had managed to extend her life for so long, to which she replied that she was in the habit of going to the synagogue early every morning. The rabbi then provided the following advice: "For three days, one after another, keep yourself away from the synagogue." The woman went off and did as he advised, and on the third day she became ill and died.[58]

The response of the rabbi in this third–century text displays a sensitivity and wisdom that often elude us today: When a person finds it too painful to live, the text teaches, it is mercifully appropriate to forgo whatever may be prolonging the pain. In this case, a life of misery was sustained by the hope and sense of belonging represented by synagogue attendance, which was perhaps the primary "treatment" at the time. In Ethel's case, a life of misery was being sustained by medical treatments that were painful in and of themselves. The point of guidance for us is that the justification for allowing death to take place is that the woman found her own life too painful to go on. In such situations, Judaism calls upon us to honor and respect the individual's preference that nature be allowed to take its course.

Acceptance of Death

Sam was an 83-year-old resident of the Alzheimer's unit of a nursing home. Despite his confusion and occasional agitation, he was a lively and sociable individual who moved around easily with a walker and seemed content with his days. Sam's condition had been stable for a year when he began a precipitous decline. Suddenly he was unable to walk or even to stand. He stared blankly into space, rarely smiled, and appeared to have lost interest in everything around him. Sam ate and drank only minimal amounts, and eventually he was hospitalized for dehydration.

In the hospital Sam received intravenous fluids, which revived him somewhat, but he still had no interest in food. He actually may have forgotten how to eat, as is often the case in the last stage of Alzheimer's disease. Doctors asked the family to consider a feeding tube, which can be inserted through the nose and down the throat or directly into the stomach. Otherwise, they said, Sam would soon die.

Sam's children deliberated for several days, anguishing over how to fulfill their duty to their father, *k'vod ha-av.* On the one hand, they were horrified by the idea that he would "starve to death" if they denied him the feeding tube. On the other hand, they imagined him being very agitated—pulling at the tube, which he would be unable to comprehend, and perhaps being put into restraints to keep him from yanking it out. It seemed cruel to put him through all of that when there really was no possibility that he would recover the ability to eat or any of the other functions he had lost. The daughter of another resident in the home had reluctantly consented to a feeding tube for her mother, who could not swallow as the result of a stroke, and she was tormented by the feeling that she had "condemned her to prison." Sam's children reminded each other that Sam had "had his life," and they accepted that his life was ending. They decided to do nothing that would interfere with the natural process of his dying.

Decisions about artificial hydration and nutrition raise questions of whether these measures are preserving and sanctifying life or hindering and prolonging the process of dying. When we turn to these measures, are we honoring our elders or condemning them to more suffering? In the case of individuals who have Alzheimer's and other types of dementia, not eating is symptomatic of the end stage of the disease. There is no evidence that feeding tubes significantly extend the lives of people with advanced dementia, and studies have shown that they actually cause physical discomfort and increased risks of aspiration and infection. Those who must decide about feeding tubes are often troubled by the idea of a loved one starving to death, which seems a cruel fate, but clinicians report that when people do not receive artificial hydration or nutrition, the body ceases to crave food and drink and adjusts to a comfortable and peaceful process of dying. In most cases the individual gradually withdraws, drifts into long periods of sleep, and requires no medication for pain.[59]

Jewish ethicists take several approaches to the question of tube feeding. The first depends on whether tube feeding is considered a form of normal food, which all would agree must be provided, or a form of artificial life support, which may be withheld or withdrawn at the end of life. Another approach focuses on tube feeding as an impediment to the natural process of dying. A third focuses on the increased discomfort and greater risk of infection, which would not be in the best interest of the individual. To liberal Jewish ethicists, all of these would be justifications for withholding or withdrawing a feeding tube.[60]

Palliative Care

As she approached the end of her life, 93-year-old Fanny was suffering from two increasingly painful conditions: osteoarthritis and congestive heart failure. The former caused so much pain that she was comfortable only when lying in bed on a special mattress, with pillows cushioning her joints. The latter condition caused painful swelling in her hands and legs as well as dangerous accumulation of fluid around her heart. Her swollen hands were bluish, her fingers hurt too much to hold a utensil, and she often begged the nurses to put her back into bed. Hospitalizations to drain the fluid from around her heart were becoming more frequent, while the benefits were diminishing.

When asked about her pain, Fanny responded that she had "had enough" and "God should take me." Her adoring family realized that she was suffering too much, and they asked that her pain be treated more aggressively. Acknowledging that neither her osteoarthritis nor her congestive heart failure was going to improve, the medical staff agreed that palliative care, or comfort measures, were the appropriate plan for Fanny. Everyone understood that the medication she needed for pain relief might weaken her lungs and her heart, and perhaps even hasten her death. In general, such a risk is ethically acceptable if the *kavana,* the intention, is not to kill the patient but to reduce her pain and suffering. However, some Jewish ethicists would limit the amount of reduction in breathing that is an acceptable side effect of pain medication.

From a Jewish perspective, palliative care is rooted in the values of *rahmanut,* compassion, *hesed,* lovingkindness, and *eyt lamut,* the acceptance of death as inevitable. Sometimes, as in Fanny's situation, it is the only way to bring about healing. The primary goal, then, is to create a situation in which a person who is terminally ill may live as comfortably as possible until the time of her death. This usually means foregoing such invasive and uncomfortable measures as feeding tubes, ventilators, or surgeries. The emphasis instead is on pain medication, social support, and spiritual care. With the patient's time and energy no longer consumed by fighting the illness, this final stage of life can be a peaceful period devoted to reflection and relationships. It can be a time of meaning, growth, and even joy.

A dilemma sometimes arises when pain cannot be adequately reduced without significant reduction of consciousness, which in turn reduces the ability to communicate and the ability to eat. Sometimes there is a choice to be made between bearing some amount of pain and losing consciousness, a decision that the patient herself should make if at all possible. Most people become alarmed when their loved ones are not eating, but the relief of pain may be more beneficial than the intake of food. Loss of consciousness affects friends and family in a variety of ways. Of course there is the distress of moving a step closer to death, but there is also the relief of seeing a loved one no longer in pain. This is one of the great benefits of palliative care. If the patient is not sufficiently conscious to make decisions about palliative care, treatment for pain is even easier to justify.

Palliative care is provided in most hospital settings and in nursing homes. It is also possible to receive palliative care through a hospice program, which specializes in comfort measures and also provides social services and spiritual support to the patient and family. Hospice care is the subject of Chapter Eight.

Variables in Pain Tolerance

For those who are making medical decisions in which pain is a factor, especially surrogate decision-makers, it is important to remember that every individual experiences pain in a unique way, depending on such variables as temperament, social situation, and religious beliefs. So what is right for one individual may be impossible for another.

A patient who is alone much of the time usually complains of more pain than a patient who has a supportive family or social network. Pain tolerance also tends to be higher among people who believe that there is a God who oversees the world and cares about all its creatures. Hope is another important factor, whether it is hope for the energy to finish a project or hope for a peaceful night's sleep. Closely related to hope is the feeling of having something to live for. Often a special event in the future, or even ongoing contact with loving family members, makes the pain worth bearing. For one whose life is devoid of supportive relationships, it is much harder to endure the pain.

So it is that two women in virtually the same medical situation could have very different responses to the pain and suffering of their disease. Ann, a 67-year-old in her first year of dialysis, complained vigorously about the treatments, sometimes even refusing to take them. Her three children did not get along with each other and were too caught up in their own issues to have much time for their mother. Ann stated that nothing in her life made the suffering worth it. She wanted to stop the treatment and be allowed to die.

Rose, a 91-year-old nursing home resident, was also in her first year of dialysis, and she complained about the strain and the inconvenience. There were many complications and bad days, but Rose never questioned whether it was all worthwhile. She wanted to live, for herself and for her family—for the daily phone calls, holiday meals, and weekend visits. Her children and grandchildren provided her with daily reminders of how much she meant to them, and their visits and calls always seemed to reenergize her. When the chaplain first heard about Rose, she was surprised that a woman in her nineties would agree to dialysis in the first place, and assumed that she would need support in discontinuing the treatments. Instead the chaplain learned something from Rose about the value of life.

Sometimes people are surprised by the decisions of those closest to them, as Dave was when he returned to the hospital the morning after his wife's doctor recommended a tracheotomy and a feeding tube. Resolved to offer Carol his support in declining the ventilator and feeding tube, he was surprised to learn that she was resolved to go ahead with both. She wanted to be around as long as she could, to continue being part of the lives of her husband and children, even in such constricted and uncomfortable circumstances. Later that day the tracheotomy was performed, and the feeding tube was inserted.

The day after the surgeries, Dave arrived at the hospital and looked sorrowfully at his beleaguered wife. She had a blue tube in her neck for breathing and a yellow tube in her stomach for nutrition. "How are you feeling today?" he asked weakly. Carol picked up the yellow pad that she kept at her side, wrote down her answer, and passed it to Dave. He was stunned by what he saw: a large number "8." From Carol's perspective—even with a feeding tube, a tracheotomy, and an incurable cancer—life was still getting some pretty high scores.

Whose Pain Is It?

When the great Rabbi Judah was dying, his disciples kept a vigil at his bedside and prayed incessantly that God not take away their beloved teacher. His maid, however, saw how much Rabbi Judah suffered and prayed to God "that the will of the immortals may overpower the mortals." As the mortals continued their prayers, she took a jar up to the roof and threw it down to the ground. The shattering of the clay interrupted the prayers of the disciples, and when they stopped praying, the soul of Rabbi Judah departed.[61]

Interpreters of this talmudic tale have praised the wisdom and compassion of the servant, who understood her master's pain. The disciples, it seems, were more focused on their own pain—the pain of losing their beloved teacher—than on the pain that he was suffering with every breath. This text reminds us how easy it is for loving and well-intentioned people to lose sight of what is in the best interest of the person who is suffering from illness and nearing the end of life. Unable to imagine life without an individual whom we love, we may protest death by embracing heroic measures, by praying incessantly for his survival, or by talking to the individual in a way that indicates our refusal to accept the impending death. Sometimes, the tale reminds us, it is more appropriate to say goodbye.

As a loved one nears death, our own emotional pain may intervene in the decision-making process. Like the disciples of Rabbi Judah, we may go to any lengths to avoid the pain of losing a loved one. Or, like his devoted maid, we may be so distressed by his suffering that we are ready to call a halt to whatever is prolonging his death. The pain of everyone involved deserves recognition and attention, but it should not divert us from honoring the needs, preferences, and best interest of the individual whose life is on the line. In this way we honor the God who gives us life, and we affirm the sanctity of the life God gives.

Rabbi Myriam Klotz

7

END-OF-LIFE CARE

Today there are many approaches to offering medical and technological assistance for the dying person, whether such assistance
be curative care intended to aggressively prolong life, or palliative care intended to help physical death ensue with the least
amount of pain and suffering. This manual examines Jewish
ethical decisions about the best possible physical care for the
dying person. When is it appropriate to remove aggressive medical
treatment and look toward helping someone die with minimal
pain? When, if, and how should the tools of modern technol-

Center for Jewish Ethics · Reconstructionist Rabbinical College

ogy be used to save or extend a life that might yet be fraught with suffering and a grim physical prognosis? Jewish tradition speaks out strongly and with nuanced sensitivity to these and other difficult decisions related to determining the best possible physical care in often impossible situations. The Jewish mandate to make choices which seek *refuat haguf,* healing of the body, is clear. There is yet another dimension involved in the care of the dying person to which Jewish core values also speak. It is addressed in various ways throughout this manual: *refuat hanefesh,* healing of the spirit. In this chapter, we focus on the concept of *refuat hanefesh,* applying an awareness of the spiritual, nonphysical dimensions of care, even while the physical body is approaching death.

In the *Mi Sheberakh* and the *refa'eynu* prayers, two central prayers in the Shabbat and daily liturgies, respectively, the petitionary language seeks *refua sh'leyma*—complete, full healing. The prayers then refine *"refua sh'leyma"* by distinguishing the overlapping and related dimensions of such healing. They continue, *"refuat hanefesh urefuat haguf"*—healing of spirit and healing of body.[62] This prayer language suggests the Jewish awareness that to experience complete healing, one must improve both physically and spiritually. The spirit, this prayer acknowledges, can become sick, just as the body can. Just as the body can heal, so too can and must the spirit of the person—even the dying person—heal from its illness, if the healing is to be complete.

It is certainly appropriate to seek a complete cure for someone whose prognosis is not terminal. Yet when considering how to tend to the possible physical healing of one who is dying, decision making does not center around curing the person. Rather, *refuat haguf* in this context involves seeking the most compassionate and incisive treatments to enable the physical body to be free of pain, thus healing from the agony of its suffering as it prepares to die. It is not, as Jewish teachings make clear, of value to endure pain when there is an alternative.[63] *Refuat hanefesh,* healing of the spirit, refers here to the ways in which one whose physical body is dying might yet move from psychological and spiritual suffering to an inner sense of wholeness, peace, and re-pose—of *menuha,* a quiet, comforting sense of rest. End-of-life care of the soul is as central a dimension of caregiving as care for the body. How does the notion of *refuat hanefesh* bear on the choices we make at the end of life? In the following pages we will look at two vital tools for offering spiritual care to the dying: *bikur holim* (visiting the sick) and healing services.

Bikur Holim: Visiting the Sick

Jewish teachings assert that it is a *mitzva,* an obligation incum-bent upon every Jew—not just the rabbi or healthcare profes-sional—to visit with those who are ill. When individuals are sick or dying, they have a natural tendency to withdraw and isolate themselves, to pull away from the web of relationships in their lives. Those who are close to the suffering person often feel hesitant about being with that person. The caregiver may fear that seeing the dying person will be difficult for both parties: the visitor might not know what to say or do; fear of dying or perhaps painful memories from past experiences might surface. The person who has had to make difficult decisions about treat-ment or procedures might feel guilty and therefore resist direct encounter. Both the dying person and the loved one, then, often have an inclination to separate; they resist moments of connection because the suffering that accompanies the journey towards death causes great emotional and spiritual pain to the one dying and to the ones witnessing that journey.

Yet the *mitzva* or sacred obligation of every Jew to practice *bikur ḥolim* suggests that the very act of being with individuals in the midst of their pain—despite the pain the visitor might experience as a result of being present—is nonetheless a sacred task and one that helps to achieve *refuat hanefesh,* healing of the spirit. Even if a family member or beloved is concerned with tasks and decisions related to immediate medical needs, this *mitzva* demands that time spent with the dying person must not only be consumed with task-oriented activities. Being simply present to the other in his or her dying fosters profound healing, even when a physical cure is impossible.

How does this *mitzva* help heal the spirit? Through the practice of *bikur ḥolim,* an empathic and open visitor can help lessen the fractured sense of self the patient might experience during the dying process. The connection during the visit reminds the dying person that the visitor still considers the patient a valued, precious person created *b'tzelem Elohim,* in the image of the eternal and limitless God. Amidst a plethora of medical practitioners whose interaction with the patient is necessarily utilitarian and goal-oriented (conduct this procedure, change that dressing, distribute this medication), the simple presence of the one visiting suggests that the dying person is not only someone who is ill. The relationship that the visit can affirm helps the dying person to remember the wholeness that is beyond the pathologies. It can restore a sense of dignity to the dying person. During the *bikur ḥolim* encounter, the glorious spirit of the dying person receives attention more than the failing body.

The practice of *hitlavut ruḥanit*—spiritual accompaniment—is at its essence what *bikur ḥolim* embodies.[64] Accompanying dying individuals on their journey by being present and attentive to them—without trying to fix or change their situation or deny its reality or busy oneself with tasks—can indeed revive a failing spirit even while a body inexorably fails. Acts of spiritual accompanying such as *bikur holim* are so important that, according to Jewish tradition, they are to be done "without limit."[65] The *mitzva* of *bikur holim* is of such importance because it invokes the inestimable value of human life, without any agenda save savoring the human connection. Unlike medical procedures or other concrete tasks that have identifiable goals and products, the goal of a *bikur holim* visit is neither quantifiable nor finite. To sit with someone without a practical agenda is to extend an act of kindness that evokes the depth of one's humanity beyond medical or technical definition. In the mysteriously simple encounter between human beings visiting with one another, there is no limit to the power of the kind words, meaningful silences, and healing moments that might be shared.

Does fulfilling an obligation for which there are no limits mean that one does not need to set limits for one's caregiving, however? Maimonides suggests in another context that people must not give so much *tzedaka* that they are then impoverished and must beg in order to survive. Similarly with the practice of *bikur holim,* one must balance between the time and energy spent in *hitlavut ruhanit* with the dying person and caring for one's own needs. Caregivers need to ensure their own endurance and health over the long term. Given the stresses of ministering to the needs of the dying, caring for oneself spiritually and physically is vital. The limitless nature of *bikur holim* refers more to the quality than the quantity of the visits. At its best, *bikur holim* means sitting through any emotional discomfort or pain that might surface during the encounter and consciously striving to remain fully attentive to subtle dimensions of the dying person's experience.

Practicing limitless presence, *hitlavut ruhanit,* through *bikur holim* does not require knowing exactly what to do and say at every juncture of the process. There is no script for this procedure. Yet some of the traditional guidelines for a *bikur holim* visit can help sensitize the visitor to the needs and realities of the dying person and can help make for an optimal encounter through which to seek a *refua sh'leyma*. The following guidelines, as explained in the medieval work Yoreh Deah, all flow from the central precept that the visitor's mission is to offer the dying person full attention, respect, and empathic caring. That applies whether one is an immediate caregiver—family, loved one, clergy, or medical professional—or one is part of the larger community of friends and colleagues who will visit the dying person to offer support.

When to Visit. According to tradition, close friends and relatives may pay a visit as soon as illness strikes, while acquaintances may visit after three days.[66] This rule recognizes with sensitivity that, despite all good intentions, it can be taxing on a patient's system to sustain contact with a wide circle of friends. Further, the rabbis suggest two instances when visitors are discouraged. First, if the sick person has a very bad headache (in this case it would cause pain to attempt to converse with the visitor), and second, if the sick person has digestive problems (and so might suffer embarrassment as a result of losing control of bodily functions).

The physical health or consciousness of a person who is dying can fluctuate greatly from day to day and hour to hour. Discernment is needed in deciding when to visit with a dying person. Tradition suggests that the best times for paying a visit are between mid-morning and late afternoon.[67] The operating principle is to be sensitive to the needs of the dying person and to plan the timing of a visit thoughtfully, so as not to interfere with possible medical treatments or sleep patterns. If there is a question, it is best to phone ahead. Visitors should be understanding if the dying person is not able to receive a visit. If it is not advisable or possible to visit in person, a phone call or card can express caring quite potently.

Length and Frequency of Visits. In general, *bikur ḥolim* visits should be frequent. A talmudic rabbi said, "One must visit up to a hundred times a day, so long as the visitor does not trouble the sick person."[68] One's spirits may be lifted again and again. If not a hundred times a day, it is nonetheless advisable to regularly let the sick persons know they are cared for and thought about. This consistency reinforces the caring social connections of the dying person. Frequent contact alleviates isolation and alienation. At the same time visitors should recognize the dying person's need and desire for privacy.

Sensitivity is needed in deciding the length of a visit. It is usually a good idea not to stay more than a short time, so as to avoid strain if the body is tired and depleted or time is needed for medical treatments.[69] Yet there may be times when it is beneficial for both caregiver and recipient that a visit be extended. Here too sensitivity toward the needs and frequently changing condition of the dying person is vital. Effective *hitlavut ruḥanit* balances the dying person's need for privacy and solitude with the need and desire for sustained, loving human contact. This attitude of caring, constant attentiveness underscores the Jewish perspective that every human being—regardless of physical state—is deserving of *kavod,* respect, and consideration for personal needs and preferences. This is an attitude that promotes *refuat hanefesh,* healing of the spirit.

Where to Sit, What to Say. Tradition states that the presence of God *(Shehinah)* rests over the head of a sick or dying person. Therefore, it is inappropriate to sit or stand over someone or to sit at the head of the bed.[70] Rather, one should try to sit beside the person. Rabbi Nancy Flam understands this teaching on a metaphorical level: "Whatever we say or do when we visit, we should make sure that we are not an obstacle to God's presence! We should not be so focused on our own agenda or desire to find the 'right' words that we fail to be present with our loved one."[71] A visitor should strive to be focused on the person being visited, humbly opening to the moments of grace that might emerge, quieting oneself to be able to deeply listen to the other. If one is struggling for what to say, s/he can simply be in silence, allowing the dying person's presence to act as a guide. Much as it might make things easier, there are no right words, no magical formula for how to deeply listen and then to sensitively respond. In fact, there is just no substitute for simple, open presence.

In many cases, the dying person wants to be honest about the situation. It is an act of caring to listen openly and to be willing to discuss the realities of dying if the person speaks about his/her impending death, even if understandable feelings of sadness, discomfort, anger, pain, or depression fill the caregiver's internal world. It is not helpful to deny the reality by changing the subject or suggesting that things will get better. It is also okay to share honestly one's own feelings in response to the loved one's terminal condition if the feelings are strongly present. If the dying person does not want to talk about the situation, as is sometimes the case, it is important not to force the issue. Again, sensitivity to the rhythms and inclinations of the dying person makes for effective end-of-life spiritual care.

The dying person might want to discuss matters that the visitor does not feel comfortable or informed enough to speak about. In response to medical questions, for example, one need not offer advice or information. Such questions or concerns are best referred to the medical team working with the person. If matters of faith or religion arise and one does not feel comfortable addressing them, a good response is suggesting that a rabbi or chaplain visit with the person to further consider these topics. The visitor's role need not be to fix, to answer, or to solve. The role is the infinitely valuable one of being simply and utterly present to the dying person.

All stages of the life cycle have challenges and opportunities. From infancy and childhood to adolescence and emerging adulthood, every person faces developmental tasks that provide opportunities to grow toward further wholeness, or *refuat hanefesh*.[72] The end of life is no exception; important opportunities for emotional and spiritual growth still exist.[73]

As a caregiver for someone who is dying, one can accompany the dying person in the journey toward growth and healing at this stage in the life cycle. Doing so means being willing to be present to the dying person's experience and to accompany the person through this time. It means being willing not to cure, not to fix, but to enter into the felt life of the person, exploring all terrain that surfaces on the journey towards death.[74]

Serving as a caregiver for someone who is dying draws forth many facets of one's humanity. Such service might evoke moments of compassion, of gentle humor, of patience, of great love. It might also elicit discomfort, fear, sadness, frustration, or pain. Such feelings and responses are natural; one is looking through the sacred window that separates the worlds of the living and the dying, between human control and surrender, between the bounded and the boundless. Feelings of grief may exist alongside conflicting emotions and thoughts about letting go. These feelings need not be denied or pushed away. Caregivers' willingness to accept the full range of their humanity in this situation can be a gift, engendering new depths of compassion and empathy for the dying person. It is important for a caregiver to seek support from others, such as counselors, friends, and clergy, if the emerging feelings become overwhelming.

The Use of Touch During a Visit. Touch is a vitally important component in the expression of caring. It can be tremendously comforting and soothing, a form of direct communication that far exceeds words in its immediacy. A visitor is encouraged to gently hold a hand or stroke a brow—but only after asking permission to do so. The dying person may be experiencing pain or discomfort that creates reluctance to experience touch. Further, the dying person has diminishing body control. Asking before touching enables the person to experience a sense of control and dignity through determining if and how touch may be received. The opportunity to choose is a liberating gift that the *bikur holim* visitor can offer.

The Role of Prayer During a Visit. Caregivers can encourage healing and the development of a dying person's spiritual life through awareness of ways that spiritual expression can take shape as one confronts the infinite and one's personal mortality. Spiritual expression may take many forms. For many people, an effective way to gain personal connection is through the act of prayer. During the last stages of life, one might turn to prayer as a way to reduce stress and pain, to find relaxation and centering, and to connect to parts of self and God not before known or perhaps desired. Prayer can thus serve as an anchor and a source of strength. Giving care to the dying includes supporting their spiritual practice, which can help prepare for dying. Even one not personally familiar or comfortable with the act of prayer can yet gently encourage a dying person's prayers. Further, traditional practice of *bikur holim* explicitly requires a visit to include prayer spoken on behalf of the sick person. What are the types of Jewish prayer one might offer and encourage during a time of *hitlavut ruḥanit* with someone who is dying?

A vast range of prayer modes is available, and some types of prayer may feel more comfortable than others at a given time. It is not necessary for the caregiver to have an active relationship to personal prayer in order to support the dying person's spiritual practice, but it is helpful to honestly assess one's relationship to prayer. Such self-reflection allows the caregiver to be open and present to the dying person's needs and practices without unacknowledged resistance or fear blocking their communication.

The classical Jewish understanding of prayer is liturgical, and involves reciting prayers from the prayer book at set times of day and night, often in a *minyan* (a group of at least ten people over the age of 13). However, other prayer experiences can also provide deep and sustaining access to the life of the spirit. Awareness of them can help the caregiver to provide resources and validation to the dying person should openness to the realm of prayer exist during spiritual preparation for death.

Petitionary Prayers. Since biblical times, Jews have poured out their hearts to God when they were in distress. Spontaneous prayers expressing hopes, anxieties, wishes, and fears have precedent in the Jewish tradition. The Psalms are rich with examples of personal prayers in which the psalmist speaks honestly to the Divine out of his personal experience, often pleading for a response. Such spontaneous prayer can be greatly therapeutic, even if the prayers are not "answered" in the manner a person might hope for. As one faces fear, pain, frustration, anger, grief or feelings of betrayal, it is of value to give voice to these emotions in a spirit of openness to God, who is acknowledged as a source full of mercy and compassion.[75] Prayers admitting personal frustrations, fears, loneliness or discomfort and seeking assistance, comfort, and release are called petitionary prayers.

Prayers of Gratitude. Jewish prayers of gratitude, or *hoda'a* prayers, fill the liturgical canon and are spoken spontaneously as well. To reflect upon the things in life for which one has felt gratitude in the past, to allow a moment of gratitude for some of the simple miracles of this present day, no matter how small they may seem—this practice can help to cultivate a state of openness to both the transitory nature of life (for who can control blessings?) and the divine eternal source from which the blessings flow. *Hoda'a* prayers can be offered at any moment in which gratitude is felt.

The Talmud[76] suggests blessing the bad experiences in life just as one should bless the good ones. This teaching points to the possibility that there is a healing aspect to holding an attitude of blessing to all of one's experience in life, and even to dying as a part of that experience. A spiritual practice can involve reflecting upon even difficult circumstances in one's situation, seeking strands of blessing that exist there, and drawing them out. The caregiver can be an encouraging presence, gently affirming an attitude of hope and meaning by articulating blessings, even in the presence of pain and loss.

Bestowal of Blessings. Another form of prayer a dying person might find helpful is offering blessings to loved ones. One of the tasks of dying involves coming to completion with others. Such completion can involve letting go of attachments, regrets, or unresolved tensions in interpersonal relationships. Conclusion also includes sharing one's last wishes, blessings, and affirmations with those who have shared the person's life. In the last chapters of the book of Genesis, there is a moving account of Jacob's dying process, where Jacob offers such blessings as he prepares to die. He gathers his sons around him and very consciously offers them a blessing one by one. Following these acts, Jacob is ready to die: "And when Jacob had finished commanding his sons, he gathered up his feet into the bed, and expired, and was gathered unto his people."[77] A sense of completion comes when one has said what needs to be said to loved ones, when one finds words of blessing.

A caregiver can support this process by acknowledging the importance and sacredness of blessings bestowed by the dying person. Some lose virtually all control by the time they are near death. Bodily functions, decisions about their treatment, and the like are no longer their own. The ability to bestow a blessing on another human being is always theirs, however, and can be a tremendously healing component of a meaningful and rich journey towards death.

Silent Prayer and Meditation. Another form of prayer involves not words, but silence. Meditation and contemplation have long been means through which people have entered into the deeper layers of the personality, experiencing such states as relaxation, ecstasy, centering, peace, and rest. Jewish mystics have developed rich practices in which the meditator focuses on the vastness beyond the known world. In that silent openness to the great beyond, one finds profound connection to the divine in the universe, and to the depths of one's own being.[78] In the repose of silence, there can be a sense of communion with the divine, with crucial insights and bits of information which the dying person needs to receive and integrate in preparing to die.

The caregiver can help the dying person cultivate permission to allow periods of silence in which inner resources are conserved and witnessed deeply, simply by demonstrating a willingness to sit in silence together. Sometimes prayerful silence can allow rich communication between caregiver and the one cared for, a communion that transcends the realm of verbal dialogue.

As mentioned, traditional laws of *bikur ḥolim* include praying by the person who visits.[79] One can feel free to offer spontaneous prayers, in silence or aloud, in the presence of the dying person or not.[80] In fact, the shortest prayer in the Bible occurs in Numbers 12:13, where Moses prays spontaneously on behalf of his sister Miriam when she is afflicted with a skin disease: "Please God, heal her now! *(El na, refa na la!)*"

Caregivers are also encouraged to utilize one of the most well-known prayers for healing in Judaism, the *Mi Sheberakh* ("The One Who Blessed") prayer. Generally speaking, this prayer is said while the Torah is open during prayers in the synagogue in both Ashkenazic and Sephardic communities.[81] In contemporary times, however, the *Mi Sheberakh* prayer has become more widely used, adapted by individuals in a variety of settings, including bedside at home, in the hospital, or in hospice.

The *Mi Sheberakh* prayer is essentially a prayer for healing. Healing is not synonymous with cure. What does it mean to pray for a full healing for someone who is dying? It asks that the dying person be blessed, as human beings in the past have been blessed, with a sense of peaceful integration *(sh'leymut)* of spirit and reconciliation of body to the dying process. The caregiver might well utilize this prayer to express personal wishes and hopes of full healing for the dying person. In the expression of this ancient Jewish prayer, the personal and immediate hopes mesh with the ancient and collective aspirations of the Jewish people for thousands of years. Such connection to the timeless essence of Judaism can provide great spiritual comfort to the dying person and to the caregiver as well.

Healing Services:
A Contemporary Form of Community Worship

"Hiney ma tov uma na'im, shevet ahim gam yahad"
("How good it is for brothers and sisters to gather together").

Psalms 133:1

In the passage from Genesis, Jacob gathered up his sons to bless them before he died. The text also says that Jacob was "gathered unto his people."[82] Judaism understands that it is important to gather together one's resources in order to best make significant change. In Jacob's case, his dying was helped when he could gather his children together around him, and in his death he was blessed to be similarly gathered to his people. As solitary as the dying process is on many levels, a Jewish perspective understands that it is also vital to have community gathered around. Such gatherings are immediate and profound ways of effecting *refuat hanefesh*. Circles or services for healing are one such mode of gathering.

Since the early 1990s, Jewish healing services have blossomed in many American Jewish communities. Such services have been inspired in large part by Rabbis Yoel Kahn and Nancy Flam, who in San Francisco crafted some of the first attempts at this emerging form. Since that time, there have been many variations and adaptations of this concept, as individuals and communities have utilized this model in their particular circumstances.[83] Many synagogues now have regular Jewish healing services that are open to the community. In these circles, participants can pray in a supportive environment for themselves or others in need of healing. The circles usually include periods of silence, time spent sharing prayers and hopes among the attendees, music, brief teaching and discussion of Torah, a ritualized washing of the hands, and a time to bless one another. Such healing services blend ancient Jewish prayers with a contemporary format.

Healing services do not replace traditional prayer services. They offer an alternative vehicle for gatherings of individuals when they are experiencing pain, suffering and loss, or are caregivers for someone in that situation. For a dying person who is well enough to attend a healing service at a synagogue, the experience can be deeply healing, providing a sense of belonging to a larger community and a supportive environment rich with prayer and song.

When a dying person is not able to attend healing services in a public setting, it is possible for caregivers to convene a healing service wherever the person is: in a hospital room, in a living room or bedroom, or anywhere else that the person will be comfortable. This event can gather together the dying person's loved ones. For example, a woman dying of cancer who had attended a monthly healing service at her local synagogue for several months was no longer able to leave her home, so the facilitators of the synagogue service made a *bikur ḥolim* visit to the woman's residence. They joined together with the woman's husband, children, brothers and sisters, and conducted a healing service in the woman's living room as she lay on the couch with an oxygen tank by her side. During this healing service, the group sang, prayed and individually expressed their love to the dying woman. Like her ancient forefather Jacob, she was able to give her blessings to the loved ones surrounding her. Soon after the healing service, she died. Her last days were enhanced by the ritualized service in which prayers, sentiments, silence and love could be gathered and shared.

As this example demonstrates, a healing service can include prayers, song, silence, and opportunities for caregivers and loved ones to offer blessings for the dying person, say goodbye and express their love. Sometimes participants bring meaningful objects to offer the dying person as a way to share the blessing and the prayer. There is room for a wide range of possibilities in constructing a Jewish healing service, since there are no formal precedents for this form of community prayer and support. It is a good idea to consult with the ill person to see what songs, prayers, or other items should be included, and who should be invited.[84]

Jewish healing services help individuals to support one another, cope with dying, and find meaning and blessing in the process. Participating in a healing service may not provide a magical cure for the dying person, but it can provide an essential part of healing care for the end-of-life period and potent memories for those who survive. In so doing, healing services help effect *refuat hanefesh,* healing of the spirit.

Finding Meaning in One's Life

Important work in preparing to die involves coming to terms with the choices and attitudes cultivated and enacted over the course of a lifetime. When people can find meaning in the lives they have led, suffering can dissipate. It can be easier to accept that one's life is complete when meaning in one's journey is recognized and affirmed.[85] A caregiver can assist this process by affirming that the dying person's life holds intrinsic meaning. At a time when one's physical sense of self is diminishing and one's identity in the world is faltering, one may need a reminder that the life journey is meaningful. The caregiver might tell the patient ways in which the patient is giving the caregiver meaning and a sense of the sacred.

Finishing Business. In this process of coming to terms with one's life, a dying person might recognize that there are pieces of business left unfinished. The caregiver can gently affirm the person's need to complete these items. Offering to help by assisting in tasks or making contacts for the person is appropriate if one feels comfortable doing so. From a Jewish perspective, *teshuva* (repentance, turning, returning) is always possible. In fact, Jews are encouraged to do *teshuva* on the day before death, according to one talmudic rabbi. Until death takes us, the gates of *teshuva* are open. It is never too late to make amends, to finish business with others, with oneself, and with God.[86]

Rabbi Amy Eilberg writes that death can be a teacher.[87] When dying is imminent, one may have the courage to examine aspects of self, of behavior, of relationships, that have not been addressed before. Utilizing the emerging awareness of impending endings, sometimes a dying person gains the desire and ability—sometimes urgently—to make amends with others and self for the past. A caregiver can affirm this activity and encourage the dying person to actively reflect upon her life and take actions resulting from these reflections.

Confession. The dying person's tasks involve achieving reconciliation on many levels. To this end, someone might experience the need for confession, for verbalizing in the presence of another person the mistakes, regrets, or sins which have not yet been brought out to air and heal. Rabbi Naḥman of Bratzlav, one of the great Hasidic masters of the 19th century, maintained that when one cannot confess one's mistakes, that awareness lodges in one's very bones.[88] Through the act of confession, one can begin to release the inner blocks to intimacy that create toxicity. One can reconcile and come to peace with the past, thus preparing the way to move into death more whole. Jewish practice affirms the importance of verbally speaking all that which has been carried internally as a burden during the course of a lifetime.

The Day of Atonement (Yom Kippur, the holiest day on the Jewish calendar), for example, is filled with moments of confession, in which Jews admit their misdeeds, own their regrets and shortcomings, and pray for reconciliation in order to move forward in their lives. Yom Kippur is in fact understood to be a day of ritualized preparing for one's own death. So, too, as the days of one's life move toward an end, Jewish perspectives encourage the confession of misdeeds as part of the attachments that have accrued during a lifetime. The caregiver can aid in the dying person's confession. One need not initiate such a conversation, but if the dying person speaks about such issues, he/she should be listened to, encouraged, and accepted.

The *Vidui* prayer is traditionally said before dying. This prayer's text involves confession, prayer for forgiveness, and ideally, coming to terms with one's life. The caregiver can make this prayer known to the dying person. If one does not feel comfortable reciting this prayer for the dying person if he or she is unable to do so, or does not feel comfortable witnessing the dying person's recital of the prayer, a rabbi or chaplain can do so. In any case, it is important to know that the Jewish tradition offers this formalized prayer as a means through which the dying person can verbally confess the failings of the past, the desire for forgiveness, and for some, the turning toward God in their preparing for death.

Forgiveness. Forgiveness—of oneself, of others, at times of God—is a related end-of-life task with which dying people might be engaged. The caregiver can encourage the dying person to open to the state of compassionate forgiveness and, if there are words that need to be spoken to another person, offer the dying person an opportunity to consider having such conversations. As caregiver, one can model hope that even at these last stages of living, change can occur through the extension of for-giveness and the cultivation of compassion in the healing of the heart.

Addressing Concerns About the Future.   In working through the tasks of saying goodbye to life, a dying person may confront difficult feelings and fears about what lies ahead. There may be fears about the dying process in terms of physical pain. A compas-sionate response from the caregiver is helpful, but it is not appro-priate to make false statements about recovery. Honestly hearing the person's concerns is a tremendous gift of authentic *hitlavut ruḥanit.*

Often a dying person will have questions about the afterlife. Is this physical life all there is? What will meet me on the other side? Does Judaism believe in an afterlife? Again, the caregiver need not expect to answer these questions, among the most poi-gnant and mysterious that a human being can ask. Simply to provide a safe and supportive context in which the person can verbalize such queries is very helpful.

That said, it is worthwhile to note that within Jewish tradi-tion are found diverse beliefs regarding whether there is an after-life and the eternal nature of the soul. The liturgy suggests that the body returns to the dust from which it came, while the soul returns to its Eternal Source. Jewish philosophers have articulated many perspectives.[89] For secular Jews, the notion that the person lives on through his or her deeds, in the memories of the sur-vivors, is pivotal. In some Jewish communities, when someone who is deceased is mentioned, the name is followed by the phrase, "May her/his memory be for a blessing." At the same time, the concept of reincarnation of the soul over lifetimes is common in Jewish mystical teachings.

As a caregiver, one can engage the dying person's inquiries

about life after death and refer the person to the wide range of Jewish commentary offered on this topic. It is not the caregiver's job to agree with the notions that the person may find meaningful; the caregiver's task is rather one of providing gentle, consistent attentiveness to the inquiry process.

Conclusion: Honoring Life, Death and Dying

In contemporary society, the process of dying can involve many painful and confusing choices engendered by advances in medical technology that render end-of-life realities complex and often not clear-cut. Further, Western culture's predominant mode of separating death and the dying process from daily life can make death a frightening bedfellow. A guiding Jewish principle is concern for the sanctity of the person who is dying, and an awareness of the needs of the whole person. End-of-life care is concerned not only with the body but with the healing and growth of the soul, the spiritual dimension of one's life. By spiritually accompanying the dying through practices of *bikur holim,* Jewish healing services, and hospice, caregivers can provide an essential and blessed element to this phase of life, reminding the dying person of the precious and eternal nature of being. These dimensions need not be overlooked, but rather honored, when focusing on medical decisions affecting the end of one's life.

Rabbi Amy Eilberg

8

A TIME TO DIE:
REFLECTIONS ON CARE FOR THE DYING

The teaching is as old as Ecclesiastes: "A time to be born and a time to die." The truth of the mortality of all living things permeates the Psalms, the *siddur* (Jewish prayer book), and all sacred text. The reality that everything must die is as ever-present as the falling of the leaves each fall and the unfolding changes in our own bodies as we age. Still, it is hard to accept. We want our time for living to stretch on without limit. And when someone we love approaches the time to die, the pain can be unbearable.

Center for Jewish Ethics · Reconstructionist Rabbinical College

I have been privileged to be with many people as their time to die approached. I have seen people suffer profoundly—physically, emotionally and spiritually—as they faced their last weeks and months of life. And I have seen people experience glimmers of great love, wisdom and even holiness, as they prepared for the end of this life. These people have taught me extraordinary lessons about death and about life, about what is real and what is possible in the final months, weeks, moments of life. My thoughts on the following pages are inspired by them, and my writing by the hope that it will bring its readers to remembering their own teachers about dying and about living, teachers who have shared their pain, their strength and their wisdom.

Hospice Care: Care of the Whole Person

My perspective on dying is profoundly shaped by the years I spent serving as a Jewish hospice chaplain. Watching hospice care providers offer care to dying people and their loved ones has forever molded my sense of what is inevitable and what is possible at the end of life.

Hospice care is care of the dying in all of its dimensions: care of the body, the psyche, and the soul offered to loved ones in their grief, fear, and fatigue. Once the desire for hospice care has been expressed by the patient or family member, indicating that the time to fight for cure has passed, the hospice team works to alleviate physical, emotional and spiritual pain, and to maximize the person's opportunity to use the remaining time with meaning, hope and love. Hospice agencies provide care either in a residential hospice facility, in a nursing home, or in the patient's own home. Hospice brings a coordinated circle of care providers—physician, nurse, social worker, chaplain, and nurse's aides and attendants as needed—to support both the dying person and his or her loved ones as they face the many challenges of the final phase of life.

In many ways, hospice care epitomizes what all medical care should be, and it exemplifies the Jewish vision of healing, addressing both *refuat hanefesh* and *refuat haguf,* the possibilities of healing of the spirit and comfort for the body, even as the hope for physical cure wanes. Hospice is care of the whole person—care of the person's body and emotions and spiritual life, care for the whole family and the person's circle of caregivers, care for the context in which the person will live the last chapter of life. Hospice care is offered by a team of providers who understand that all parts of the person are interconnected, and that these connections must be honored.

With hospice care, the focus shifts from the search for one more treatment to the process of reducing suffering and helping the person to live the time remaining in the richest possible way. Hospice is care that is loving, fierce in its determination to alleviate pain, and respectful of the life this person has lived. Hospice, at its best, is care that is unafraid of death and pain, reverent of the mysteries of life and death, and aware of the limitations of medical technology and of the possibilities of love.

The Needs of the Dying

Every stage of life has its own challenges and opportunities. Babies learn to live in the world, to receive nourishment, to trust and to love; toddlers learn to walk and talk; adolescents learn to develop their own unique identities. People who know that death is near have enormous challenges to face, and sometimes, still, possibilities for learning, growing, and healing.

In a host of ways, hospice care specifically addresses the needs, fears, and challenges that dying people face. Hospice specializes in the aggressive treatment of physical pain. But hospice workers also address other primary realities of dying people: loneliness and fear and grief. Dying people need to talk, to review their lives, to look back and celebrate the gratifying parts of this life, to acknowledge, grieve and, when possible, make peace with the painful parts of the lives they have lived. Dying people need to grieve—to express the whole range of feelings that the dying process evokes; people need to be heard and soothed and comforted. This kind of listening and witnessing is at the essence of hospice care.

Dying people need to address unfinished business in their lives: from financial affairs to care of loved ones to seeking reconciliation in broken relationships. In hospice, those who have the strength and desire receive support for exploring ways to heal relationships and to receive forgiveness—from themselves, from others, or from God. Many dying people feel a strong need to leave behind a legacy of their lives. Hospice staff regularly facilitate the creation of tapes and memory books, which are a priceless treasure for loved ones left behind. Hospice people know how to affirm people's sense that their lives had meaning, that they will be remembered for blessing. Many dying people need to make plans for their own funerals. Hospice workers can support people in this awesome task, understanding that this can be a wonderful way to take charge of what is still in one's control.

It seems to me that for the vast majority of people, the final chapter of life is full of pain, fear and grief. Yet sometimes, too, there are moments of beauty, times when it seems that everything will be okay, that we are cared for, that life is just as it should be, and that loved ones are precious. It takes a person unafraid of death to deeply share such moments with a dying person. Hospice programs are full of staff people who know how to listen in this way.

People who have seen a dying process accompanied by hospice care often learn again what the rabbis taught long ago. As the rabbis said, it is possible (even imperative) to do *teshuva* on the day before we die—to turn our lives around, to atone for sin and seek and receive forgiveness, to turn peacefully toward ourselves, our loved ones, and God, no matter how little time remains. Hospice care helps people to live the final stage of life in just this spirit, with as much comfort, richness, and holiness as possible.

Jewish Concerns about Hospice Care

With such extraordinary care available to soothe and enrich the final days and weeks of life, why is it still so hard for many families to choose hospice care? There are many reasons why people may resist the inevitable. One major factor, of course, is denial of death. Consumers of American culture often worship youth and immortality, influenced by a culture increasingly convinced of its own power over nature. Many people still struggle mightily to accept the reality that death is near. And of course, fear can keep us from seeing clearly that the time to prepare for death has come. For all of this, one need not be Jewish. But in my experience, hospice-care providers around the country express concern that Jewish families have an even harder time choosing hospice than other religious and ethnic groups. What keeps Jews, in particular, from choosing hospice?

Jewish Tradition. For some, the answer lies in interpreting Jewish tradition and understandings of what *halakha* teaches about care for the terminally ill. In my experience, a remarkable percentage of Jewish families know that Jewish tradition values life above all, and that one must fight for life at all costs.

In fact, there is a substantial basis for this view in classical Jewish sources. It is well known that according to *halakha* the preservation of life takes precedence over all *mitzvot,* with only three exceptions: the prohibitions against adultery, idolatry, and murder. In stark distinction to contemporary American reflections on the individual's quality of life, Jewish tradition teaches that "the lives of people are not their property, but the property of the Holy One."[90]

Consider, too, the classical view of all of the ancient law codes regarding the exquisite, life-supporting care to be provided to a *goses,* a person expected to die within three days. One may not close the eyes of a dying person *(goses);* one who touches him so as to move him is a murderer.[91]

A dying person *(goses)* is considered to be alive in every respect. . . . To what may s/he be compared? To a flickering flame, which is extinguished as soon as one touches it. Whoever closes the eyes of the dying while the soul is about to depart is shedding blood. One should wait a while; perhaps s/he is only in a swoon.[92]

Nonetheless, the following source from the 12th century work of ethics and theology, the *Sefer Hasidim,* conveys a very different perspective: "'There is a time to be born and a time to die.' (Ecc. 3:2) Why did Kohelet say this? With respect to one who is dying, a *goses,* we do not cry out on his behalf [in the hope] that his soul will return. He can at best live only a few days, and in those days he will suffer greatly. Thus it says, 'a time to die.'"[93]

Based on this, on a number of statements in the sources of Jewish law, and on the values that liberal Judaism espouses, liberal Judaism has long permitted the termination of treatment offered to a terminally ill patient under certain circumstances. Many authorities believe it is the sacred duty of a life-affirming tradition to recognize and honor the moment when the time has come to die. Even clearer, in their view, is the case of hospice, which is not a choice to terminate treatment at all but a choice to shift the focus of medical care from the pursuit of cure to the management of pain and the offer of comfort.

Rabbi Elliot Dorff, an eminent scholar of the Conservative movement, has compellingly challenged the view that Jewish law insists on maintaining life under all circumstances. The tradition, after all, considers capital punishment to be a possibility; the tradition affirmatively teaches that a Jew may kill another in order to protect his or her own life; and the tradition teaches that we are to allow ourselves to be killed rather than commit acts of idolatry, adultery or murder.

Thus, while Jewish tradition unquestionably has a passionate and overriding concern with the preservation of life in most situations, Jewish tradition nonetheless grants the patient a significant degree of autonomy in choosing among several medically justifiable courses of treatment. A close reading of Jewish legal texts reveals that the patient is entitled to reject even potentially effective treatments, if their risks or side effects are unbearable to him/her. In the view of one classical commentator, the patient may reject treatments that are not *"letovato"*—not to his benefit—as this person experiences it.[94] Or, as another source puts it, "The heart knows its own bitterness," asserting that only the patient may know which treatments he or she can tolerate.[95]

Dorff's analysis suggests that the patient has a right to choose among medically justifiable courses of treatment. Thus, to choose hospice care is not to reject treatment, not to neglect the care of the body that is entrusted to us by God. On the contrary, while the patient may choose to undergo painful and risky treatments in the continuing hope for cure, the patient may choose to reject such treatments as excessively painful and essentially hopeless, and choose instead the form of medical care that most directly addresses the many needs of the person facing death.

Dorff's ringing endorsement of hospice care has been echoed by many rabbinic authorities across the spectrum of Jewish life:

> As we learn more about the dying process, hospice care be-comes not only a permissible option, but, at least in most cases, the Jewishly preferable one. . . . It has become widely known that dying patients usually do not fear death as much as they fear pain, isolation, physical deterioration, and infantilization. Therefore hospice care . . . has a much better chance than a hospital does of addressing the real needs of the dying. . . . Even the person's physical needs are probably better served through hospice care. One enters a hospice program fully aware that death cannot be avoided; therefore the goal of both the person and the attending health care personnel is no longer confused by unrealistic wishes but is rather clearly focused on pain management. Since Judaism generally is interested in the whole person and not just the body, and since even care of the body is greatly influenced by a person's psychological well-being, rabbis should explore it [hospice care] with the terminally ill and their families, and where appropriate, recommend it.[96]

Jewish Attitudes toward Death. If in fact there is a significant consensus of belief among eminent Jewish scholars that hospice is a Jewishly defensible and even preferable choice, why the low rate of hospice utilization among Jews? If Jewish law and Jewish values are not a reason to reject hospice care, why is it so hard for Jews to make the choice for hospice?

After years of working with Jewish families struggling with

the agonizing process of caring for a dying loved one, I see that Jews struggle, like everyone else, with denial and fear, with grief and uncertainty in the face of death. And specifically for Jews, certain attitudes toward death are deep in the Jewish collective consciousness, shaped and reinforced throughout Jewish history.

Death as the Enemy. For many Jews, death is an enemy to be vanquished at all costs. The determination to defeat death feels like the ultimate *mitzva,* the very essence of Jewish identity. The knowledge that the Jewish people has fought off one despotic threat after another throughout our history, and continued against all odds to thrive, lives at the core of Jewish identity for many of us. Perhaps Jewish teaching would have proclaimed that life is an ultimate value even if the Jewish people had undergone a different journey through history. But that piece of classical teaching took on visceral meaning, so that many Jews—long since removed from Jewish ritual practice or traditional learning—know in their cores that to be Jewish is to fight death valiantly, no matter what.

Unfortunately, this collective story of survival, so essential to Jewish continuity and pride, translates imperfectly into the life of the individual Jew. I have seen many a person struggling in the last days and weeks of life to maintain that fierce determination to defeat death that seems, as it were, to be written into the collective Jewish DNA. When I see a young mother marshalling every ounce of energy to thwart death's plan, I thank God for this force within us that moves us to fight for life. When I see an older person repeatedly defying medical expectations, determined to live the last chapter of life with power, grace, and individuality, I see the extraordinary blessing of the passion for life programmed within us.

But I have seen people missing opportunities to put their

last days and weeks to good use because they felt they had no choice but to fight to the very end. I have seen people suffer deeply as they threw every shred of energy into outsmarting death. I have seen people miss the chance to say goodbye, to say "I'm sorry," to say "I love you," because on some level they did not have the help they needed to learn—not just in theory but for themselves—that just as there is a time to be born, so too there is a time to die. This is not the only Jewish way—and not even the most authentically Jewish way—to view death. When read carefully, our rich tradition offers us other ways to regard the place of death in life.

Death as a Part of Life. One can open almost any classical Jewish book and find evidence of a Jewish attitude toward death very different from the "death as an enemy" approach that is so common among American Jews and so consonant with the view of secular American culture. By contrast, the view of death that is best represented in classical Jewish sources is that death is a part of life, a part of God's creation.

Jewish tradition is rich with texts that cultivate our awareness of mortality as a part of the divine plan for humankind. Death is as predictable a part of living as being born and growing, as well as a necessary end to a life well-lived. Jewish sources that cultivate this perspective emphasize God's role as Creator and the immenseness of God and the Universe in contrast to the short span of human life. Somehow, there is some comfort in this: this is the way life is supposed to be—full and rich, and finite.

Consider, for example, the following classic statement from Psalm 90:

Your sleep, [O God] engulfs all mortals.
They flourish for a day, like grass.

In the morning it sprouts afresh;
by nightfall it fades and withers. . . .
Three score and ten our years may number,
four score years if granted the vigor.
Laden with trouble and travail,
Life quickly passes and flies away. . . .
Teach us to use all of our days,
that we may attain a heart of wisdom. . . .

Or consider the following less well-known midrash from
Kohelet Raba (7:4). The midrash reflects on the puzzling verse
from Ecclesiastes, "A good name is better than fine oil; the day
of death is better than the day of birth" (7:1).

The day of death is better than the day of birth? For Americans this is a particular puzzle. We celebrate birthdays; we celebrate birth—and rightly so—as a time of joy, of promise, of
awareness of miracles. Death is a time of grief, confusion, and
bitterness. This midrashic author reverses our usual understanding, using the metaphor of a ship's journey. Most people, he says,
celebrate when a boat sets off to sea and offer no acknowledg-
ment when the boat returns safely home. "When a ship sets out
from harbor," says the midrashist,

> one never knows what storms it may encounter, what obstacles
> may impede its journey. It is when the ship returns safely and
> successfully at the end of the journey that one does well to
> celebrate. So, too, it is at the end of life's journey, when one
> knows that life has been well lived. That is the time for satis-
> faction, for peace, even for celebration.

Our tradition, in its wisdom, understands profoundly how
much pain death can leave in its wake. Yet this midrash em-

bodies a truth worth pondering: that the essence of life can be known most fully at its end rather than at its start, that in fact, life's finitude is a part of its beauty.

Death as a Teacher. Over the years I have come to believe that Jewish practice teaches yet another perspective on the place of death in life. It seems that there are lessons that some of us learn best when we are in close contact with the reality of death. When we have no choice but to recognize that life is finite, that we and everyone we will ever love will die, we are often catapulted into an intense experience of the preciousness of life.

Death can be a teacher about the fragility of life and its beauty, about the deep importance of loved ones and of treasured values, about the ways in which life gives us extraordinary gifts, that even loss sometimes brings blessing in its wake. Death is a teacher about God's presence in the world, about human goodness and compassion and love. Death is a teacher about courage and hope and faith, about believing in that which we cannot see, about moving through the valley of the shadow until light is visible again.

Embedded in Jewish liturgy are references to death that can be understood as death-awareness practices, rituals that specifically direct our attention to the fact of our own mortality. These prayers, recited daily over a lifetime, offer the chance to cultivate the capacity not only to tolerate the reality of death, but to embrace its teachings throughout our lifetime—until, perhaps, our own final moments.

Consider the fact that traditional Jews recite the *Shema* every night before going to sleep. It is surely no coincidence that the *Shema* is also to be recited just before death. In instituting these practices, the rabbis almost certainly intended to have us treat the process of going to bed each night as a daily rehearsal for the final moments of life. Each night, we relinquish our conscious control over our lives. We descend into darkness, into a state in which we have little control over our bodies or our thoughts, a state that the rabbis called a sixtieth part of death. Each night, we place our lives in the hands of God—just as we will when we close our eyes for the last time. Each night, we are to practice trusting that somehow, without our knowledge or control, everything will be okay. Atheists too place their trust in the universe because all of us need sleep.

Then upon first awakening in the morning, the traditional Jew recites the words, "*Modeh/modah ani lefanekha . . .* I thank you, Ever-living God, that you have returned my soul to me in love. Your faithfulness is very great." Such Jews begin each morning with the awareness that the soul placed in God's care the previous night has been returned, as a loving gift, once more this morning. It seems clear that the rabbis hoped that a lifetime of beginning and ending our days with the awareness of the precious gift of life would condition us to live differently and perhaps when the time came, die just a little differently. Far from an enemy to be denied or vanquished, death can be a teacher about the preciousness of life.

Someday, perhaps, it will be better understood that Jews need not always fight valiantly to the very last moment of life. Someday, perhaps, more Jews will recognize that dying people can be offered specialized pain relief, comfort, and deep companionship at this very sacred time of life, and that life can be savored right up to the end. Someday, perhaps, more Jews will understand that a lifelong journey of learning and growing and loving can continue, as the rabbis said, until the day before we die, or even to the moment of death itself.

9

ENDING LIFE

Life and Death

Judaism is life-intoxicated, as Rabbi Harold Schulweis says. We toast *l'chaim!* to show our dedication to life. The Shulḥan Arukh reminds us that "one hour in this world is better than the entire world to come." We believe in the joy and sanctity of life, and we celebrate it as the most precious gift God has bestowed on us.

Not only may one violate Shabbat and virtually all other

commandments to save a life, one is *obligated* to do so. Maimonides, in fact, charges that rabbis or other community leaders must themselves violate the Shabbat to save someone's life. They may not arrange for non-Jews or less educated Jews to violate Shabbat for them, for all should see that saving a life, even while violating Shabbat, is a most sacred obligation.

Yet Jews have always recognized how finite and precious is our fleeting time on earth. We recognize that life naturally reaches an end point. Though Jews have always had a reverence for life, our tradition neither denies nor reveres death. Judaism reacted against Egypt's cult of death, understanding that though death represents a transition, it is not itself to be overtly worshipped or desperately feared. Nor do we have all the answers about the unfathomable nature of death; the great Rabbi J. B. Soloveitchik confessed: "At times I am given over to panic; I am afraid of death. At other times, I am horrified at the thought of becoming, God forbid, incapacitated during my lifetime. I don't know what to fear, what not to fear: I am utterly confused and ignorant."

The reverence for life, sacrifice in the service of maintaining life, and humility before life's mysteries guide Judaism's approach to the end of life. If life itself is so profoundly and ultimately sacred, how could we ever consider intentionally cutting any life short, even a life of pain and suffering?

And yet the questions seem less simple when one is standing at the bedside of a loved one. Unfortunately, the concluding stage of life is often accompanied by physical pain, emotional anguish, and psychological suffering, all of which Judaism also takes very seriously. People are often faced with a decision, a decision that they do not want to make, but must. We may see the loss of the personhood that made our loved one so ultimately precious to us. The one we once loved may now be little more than a body, with no "self" inside that we can fathom. Or the body and mind may still be alert but fighting a losing battle amidst overwhelming pain and suffering. Our loved one may be telling us that the fight has ended, that he or she is ready to go.

Where does the *mitzva* lie? Is the *mitzva* to stop treatment, to recognize that life itself has ceased to be life, that we can ease the transition into the next world through an act of *rahmanut,* compassion? Do we sit and watch our loved one suffer? Could it be a *mitzva* to have the power to stop suffering and yet do nothing? Or is life itself so sacred that we must protect it at all cost, like a delicate crystal buffeted about by the storms of disease and infirmity?

Such questions are not new to our heritage, though they take on new meaning in a technological age. The rabbis have asked these questions for literally thousands of years, and each new generation struggles with their meaning. Today, these questions take on a new urgency, for now the questions are not the exception but the rule. How should a Jew respond, as life draws to a close, to the challenges and benefits of modern medical technology?

The Basic Question of Ending Life

Traditionally, the rabbis have interpreted Judaism as clearly opposed to suicide or euthanasia in almost all cases. However, a closer inspection of the tradition finds exceptions, and surprising latitude when one is suffering. The cases discussed in Jewish tradition are based on the idea that medicine can no longer help the suffering person; today, it is medicine itself that often maintains life to the point that suffering becomes intolerable. We can find within Jewish tradition great sympathy for taking measures to reduce or end suffering at the end of life.

Still, Judaism has a reverence for life that forbids taking such measures cavalierly. A person who is dying comfortably, or who is not in pain, or who is in pain but is still able to enjoy many of the pleasures life bestows—the visits of family, favorite foods, Jewish ritual—clearly is not a candidate for the kinds of measures discussed in this chapter. Hastening the end of life should never be done for the convenience of the family, or because the family members would "never want to live like that," if the dying patient does not desire a hastening of death.

Similarly, patients who are depressed or otherwise psychologically or cognitively unable to make such a decision must first be treated until they are capable of decision making before their end-of-life desires should be considered valid. Dr. Jack Kevorkian, who raised the issue of physician-assisted suicide in American society, has often been criticized for not assuring the mental fitness of the patients he helped to die before agreeing to aid them. However, it is also important to remember that the end of life is often a time of great emotional and mental turmoil, and the natural sadnesses and difficulties of dying should not be overinterpreted as psychiatric problems that discount a dying patient's needs and desires.

People have different tolerances for pain and anguish. Only the patient knows his or her true suffering. "The heart knows its own bitterness," Proverbs 14:10 tells us. There are those who live and enjoy life under circumstances that many of us, looking in from the outside, might consider intolerable. In fact, the group that is the most opposed to physician-assisted suicide in the United States is called Not Dead Yet. It is a group of disabled people, many confined for their entire lives to wheelchairs or beds. They enjoy their lives, yet are often told by able-bodied people, "How can you enjoy life like that? I'd want to kill myself!" They worry that if physicians are allowed to help people die, everyone will assume that they will want to be the first to go. In polls of happiness and life satisfaction, the disabled often score higher than able-bodied people, and the infirm higher than those who are well. Furthermore, people who were able-bodied and then became injured or severely ill often say that they never could have imagined in advance what that life would be like. We should never assume that we know what life is like for another, or that a loved one does not want to live simply because others imagine that they would not want to live under those conditions.

However, there are those near the end of life who clearly feel that their lives are not worth living because of intractable pain, loss of dignity, loss of capability, or other difficulties. There are those who repeatedly and actively ask for help in committing suicide or dying, and are clearly lucid and understand what their requests mean. There are those whose lives have become a long, drawn-out, and painful dying and who are no longer able to clearly communicate their wishes. There are those drifting towards their death with only life supports keeping them from taking their final journey.

How should Jews respond to these challenges? Is it acceptable to remove life-support systems from a dying person? Is it justifiable, in Judaism, to actively help someone die? Does Judaism see something noble in suffering, some divine opportunity for growth or learning? Does Judaism believe God wants us to suffer upon our deaths?

The question of whether the dying can be helped to die is not new to Judaism. The Talmud uses the term *goses* (see Chapter 6) to refer to someone moribund or imminently dying, usually defined as someone who will die within three days. There is also the idea of the *t'refa* (see Chapter 6), someone who is terminally ill and will die within the year. Jewish tradition treats these two categories differently and, as we struggle to understand how we should think about deciding to end life, it may be instructive to look at them briefly.

There is an argument in some modern Jewish scholarship over whether we should look for guidance concerning today's dying patients through the model of the *goses* or the *t'refa*.[97] The *goses* is one who is imminently dying; the *t'refa* has a terminal illness but may live for considerably longer. Traditional sources tell us that we may not cause the *goses* to die or do anything that hastens death. To "close the eyes" of a *goses* (that is, while still alive), as one does to a corpse, is like shedding blood. On the other hand, we *may* remove "impediments" to death, something that keeps the *goses* from dying naturally.[98] Discontinuing respirators and feeding tubes is today most often understood as removing impediments to dying, not as causing death. The tradition also suggests we have a positive obligation not to unnaturally prolong death in the case of the *goses*. Clearly the model of the *goses* suggests that we can remove impediments, but not actively cause the death of another.

However, other scholars suggest that modern dying fits more into the category of the *t'refa,* one who is clearly and severely terminally ill. One who kills a *t'refa* is exempt from (earthly) punishment. The idea of the *t'refa,* therefore, broadens the allowability of removing life supports and even nutrition and hydration at the end of life. Pain management, even if it shortens life, is certainly permitted.

Modern liberal Judaism uses these ideas as guideposts to decision making. The underlying intention of the *goses* and *t'refa* discussions is to maintain the dignity of the dying, and not to unduly hasten their deaths; on the other hand, that obligation is tempered with mercy and a recognition that death is also part of the rhythm of human existence. The decision of the family to end life support, when done in a reflective and respectful way, is also a great *mitzva*.

Assisted Suicide.

Traditional Jewish sources have always condemned suicide, yet they understand the difficulties of pain and suffering. As a result, they define suicide extremely narrowly. The practical results are that Jewish tradition allows great latitude in ending life without labeling it "suicide." Within the general disapproval of suicide are openings for a more permissive view of how to treat end-of-life care.

Suicide is forbidden traditionally for a number of reasons. One view is that God owns our bodies, that we are only the guardians of our bodies for our time on earth; therefore, we have no right to destroy what does not belong to us. A second line of reasoning suggests not that God has divine authority over our bodies, but rather that they are the source of supreme value, being created *b'tzelem Elohim,* in the image of God. They must therefore be protected and safeguarded. Judaism also recognizes that suicide in general is painful for those who are left behind, and that it is ultimately a social, not an individual act.

While the three largest branches of Judaism oppose suicide of any kind, there is also great sympathy and understanding for those who are driven to such desperate measures. As a Reform responsum comments, there is in Jewish law a "distinction between *Lehatkhila,* 'doing an action to begin with,' and *Bedi-avad,* 'after the action is done.' Thus, we do not say that *Lehatkhila* it is permissible for a man to ask for death, but *Bedi-avad,* if under great stress he has done so, it is forgivable."[99]

In fact, the Talmud tells us that Rabbi Judah asks: "How could Zedekiah, aware that the strangers would pierce his eyes, not have had the sense to dash his head against the wall until life left him?"[100] Rabbi Judah seems to take it for granted that the potential for great suffering allows for the possibility of suicide. However, the suicide of King Saul is the event that evokes the most serious and nuanced discussion of suicide in the Jewish tradition:

> The battle raged around Saul, and some of the archers hit him, and he was sorely wounded by the archers. Saul said to his arms-bearer, "Draw your sword and run me through, so that the uncircumcised may not run me through and make sport of me." But his arms-bearer, in his great awe, refused; whereupon Saul grasped the sword and fell upon it.

The death of Saul has been debated at length by the rabbis. Some suggest he committed suicide to avoid his capture and torture, which would dishearten his people, as they were engaged in war. Others suggest he feared that torture would force him to renounce God, thus becoming an apostate. Suicide is considered acceptable rather than committing idolatry (the only other suicides praised by the rabbis are those of Hananiah, Misha'el, and Azariah, who chose death rather than worshiping idols). Others suggest that Saul was indeed fearful of physical suffering, and thus was under the sway of powerful emotions that rendered his suicide excusable (for he was not in his right mind), though not praiseworthy. And finally there are those, like the great scholar Naḥmanides, who suggest that Saul was in a dire situation with no escape, and that suicide is acceptable under those circumstances.[101]

Is illness itself not a kind of dire situation with no escape, one that will ultimately kill us? Might our pain and suffering not also be akin to torture, putting the dying person at risk—as with Saul—of renouncing God? If we interpret the experience of Saul as a fear of physical torture, as a recognition of a

dire situation from which there is no escape, then Jewish tradition leaves room to accept the decision to take one's own life
as disease begins to hold the body hostage.

In the United States, the State of Oregon is the only one
that permits physician-assisted suicide. The Oregon law allows
doctors to prescribe a lethal dose of drugs to patients, who can
then fill the prescription and use it to end their own lives. The
law stipulates that the patient must have been certified by two
physicians to have less than six months to live, that he or she is
of sound mind, and has made a written request to die.[102] Polls
of public opinion found that Jews were more likely than most
other groups to support people's right to choose physician-
assisted suicide. So there is, among Jewish people, a strong sympathy for the right to end suffering, even if it means intentionally
ending life.

Is physician-assisted suicide finally acceptable in Judaism?
While Judaism does not fully condone suicide, Jewish tradition
finds reasons not to condemn it. Those drawn to it because of
their suffering are, like King Saul, in a dire situation with no
other escape. In such situations, the decision to end one's life
must be received with compassion and understanding.

Euthanasia and End-of-Life Care

It is not assisted suicide, but some form of euthanasia that confronts most caretakers, pastoral counselors, and patients at the
end of life. The word euthanasia originated from the Greek language: *eu* means "good" and *thanatos* means "death." The word
has come to mean active intervention to end a person's life so
as to reduce physical or mental suffering.

For many years, the modern discussion of euthanasia differ-
entiated between passive and active euthanasia. Today, most

bioethicists reject the difference, finding the terms ultimately confusing and difficult to differentiate. Still, they are commonly used by doctors and people facing end-of-life decision making, and traditional Judaism clearly differentiates between them.

- *Passive euthanasia* occurs when medical interventions, like ventilators or feeding tubes, are removed from a dying patient to allow the natural process to follow its course.

- *Active euthanasia* occurs when the physician or another person does something, such as giving a patient a drug, that directly causes death sooner than it otherwise would occur.

Passive Euthanasia. A famous story in the Talmud tells of the great Reb Yehuda Hanasi, Judah the Prince, who was dying. His disciples stood around him and prayed for his life. His chambermaid also prayed for his life, until she saw what pain and hardship he suffered as he tried to rise and move about. She changed her prayer, hoping that God would allow his death. But the prayers of the disciples held death at bay. So she took a chamberpot and dropped it; at the moment of its shattering, the disciples were distracted, and death took the soul of Yehuda Hanasi.[103]

The chambermaid was responsible for allowing the death of the great man. Should she be condemned? To the contrary, the rabbis praise her for her actions. The disciples, many rabbis comment, were putting an unacceptable impediment in the way of dying. The Shulḥan Arukh says that if a man is dying in his home, and the sound of a woodchopper outside his window is keeping him from finally passing, the woodchopper may be stopped.[104] It is acceptable to remove things that keep a person from a natural death.

The tradition looks at removal of these impediments in a

beautifully deep and careful way: A midrash tells of an elderly woman who went to Rabbi Yose ben Halafta saying that she was so old that life had no more meaning, that she had lost her desire to live and wanted to leave the world. The rabbi asked how she had managed to live to such a ripe old age, and she replied that she prayed in her synagogue every morning. "Absent yourself from the synagogue for three consecutive days," the rabbi suggested. The woman followed his advice, and on the third day she died.[105]

What are we to make of this story? It is important to recognize that the woman's suffering is taken very seriously by Yose, even though it is suffering of the spirit and not of the body. He takes it so seriously that he agrees at some level that she is better off dying than living like that. So he helps her find a way to die —by removing the activity that is keeping her alive, even though it is an important and desirable activity.

We can learn from this, first of all, that suffering at the end of life, even suffering of the spirit, is taken with utmost seriousness in Judaism, and that measures can be taken to end it. But what of the idea of the *goses,* that we may not hasten the dying of a person who is at the end of life? Looked at today, the *goses* prohibition cautions us about a premature, unnecessary disruption of the dying process. The concept of *goses* reminds us that while a breath of life exists in us, the spirit of God is present, and there is no reason to hasten death for its own sake. We are quick to want to "put people out of their misery," to end suffering. It is a noble desire. But life itself has a value in Judaism that must be weighed against suffering; we do not end life easily, or simply because the end is near. On the other hand, all methods of alleviating pain are permitted. When pain is reduced as far as possible, the suffering may well be constrained enough to make the process of dying much more bearable.

It is generally accepted in Judaism that when life is inevitably going to end and patient suffering is great, all impediments to dying may be removed. Ventilators may be disconnected, drugs ceased, procedures stopped, DNR orders instituted. The *goses* is not supposed to be touched even to help; that is, the Talmud understood that there is a moment when all intervention is over, and when we should simply be with the dying. The concept that we are not supposed to touch the *goses* can help people through this painful moment. Though people may feel guilt that they are "deciding to let mother die," ultimately it is seen in Judaism as an act of *raḥmanut,* compassion.

Active Euthanasia.   The Talmud tells the story of the martyr-dom of Rabbi Ḥanina ben Teradion at the hands of his Roman torturers, who burned him at the stake. His executioners

> . . . wrapped him in a Torah scroll, surrounded him with bundles of vine shoots, and set them on fire. They brought tufts of wool, soaked them in water, and placed them over his heart, so that his soul would not depart quickly. . . . His disciples said to him, "Open your mouth, so that the fire will enter you quickly!" Rabbi Ḥanina replied: "It is better that it be taken by the One who has bestowed it [God]—a person should not harm himself."
>
> The executioner said to him: "Master, if I increase the flames and remove the tufts of wool from over your heart, will you bring me into the life of the world-to-come?" "Yes." "Swear to me!" Rabbi Ḥanina swore to him. The executioner then increased the flames and removed the tufts of wool from over his heart, and Rabbi Ḥanina's soul departed quickly. The executioner forthwith threw himself into the fire; a divine voice announced: "Rabbi Ḥanina ben Teradion and his exe-cutioner are assigned to life in the world to come."[106]

The rabbi refused to open his mouth and hasten his death, for according to the Talmud, one may not injure oneself. However, the Talmud clearly allows the removal of an impediment to death—the tufts of wool. But the most fascinating part of the story, and one commentators have not dealt with in sufficient depth, is that the executioner *increases the flames,* thus doing something proactive to hasten death. Yet, according to the story, he is still given a place in the world to come.

The Rabbi Ḥanina story includes an element of active euthanasia, of taking an action that directly hastens death. Again, as in suicide, the door remains open to actions that, in general, are not permitted by Jewish law. The wisdom of the tradition is in its understanding of the complexity of human life, of the necessity of applying laws and guidelines with flexibility and humanity, and the need to understand that ultimately, "the heart knows its own bitterness."

The Final Decision

The stories of Saul, of Rabbi Ḥalafta, and of Rabbi Ḥanina show that the inevitable decisions at life's end are not simple. All three stories are morally ambiguous and full of anguish, displaying the difficulty of deciding how best to cope with choices about ending life more quickly, more easily, more painlessly.

The specifics of individual cases can only be decided one at a time. How much technology should be removed as an impediment to dying and when it can be removed are matters subject to different interpretations among bioethicists and rabbis. Decisions in individual cases should be made by the patient or the patient's proxy, with the consultation of the family, doctor, rabbi, or other trusted advisors. Clearly, when hope is gone and dying has begun, removing medications, artificial means of bodily functions, and extraordinary measures of keeping a person alive is a compassionate act well in keeping with Jewish tradition.

Decisions made within the spirit of human caring and Jewish ethics that have the medical and spiritual welfare of the dying patient firmly as the top priority are all touched ultimately by the presence of God.

Richard Hirsh

10

DEATH AND MOURNING

Few moments in human life carry as much meaning as those that touch on the boundaries of life. Jewish rituals and observances can help guide us through such boundary moments. At times of transition, traditions, values and customs can help create meaning and structure as well as provide comfort.

Life-boundary moments can be disruptive and disturbing, and death in particular is destabilizing. Death makes us aware of the inevitable and universal transience of life, and alongside

Center for Jewish Ethics · Reconstructionist Rabbinical College

our sorrow we hear the echo of our own mortality that accompanies moments of grieving and memorializing.

The purpose of this chapter is to suggest basic Jewish practices that can serve as spiritual resources for mourners and for those who comfort mourners. A guide is not a code; it does not prescribe what each individual should do. A guide is, instead, a pathway through Jewish tradition that provides explanations, illuminates values and suggests approaches that are responsive to the needs of contemporary Jews.

This chapter reflects two fundamental commitments:

- *fidelity* to the customs and traditions of the Jewish people, for each generation of Jews is the custodian of Judaism and bears the responsibility of ensuring its preservation and transmission;

- *responsiveness* to the needs of contemporary Jews, reflected in a willingness to adapt and innovate.

From a traditional as well as a contemporary perspective, many Jewish practices associated with mourning are subject to local adaptation and the customs of differing communities. What may be standard in one locale would not necessarily be done elsewhere. While the decision regarding which rituals and customs to observe is the responsibility of each mourner, a rabbi can help provide information and insight as to what is essential and what is marginal, what is recommended and what is discouraged. A rabbi can also help identify the general patterns of observance within a community as a way of providing communal guidance to individual mourners.

Explanations for rituals vary widely. Traditions surrounding death and mourning are in many cases centuries old, and the origins of customs are usually obscure, although some explanations are accepted as normative. This chapter affirms the possibility of reading new meanings into old rituals while preserving those rituals out of a sense of continuity and commitment.

Because death is so profoundly disorienting, we are often eager to make use of as much of our tradition as possible to help us cope with loss. Previous patterns of personal and/or family ritual observance may be minimal, but mourners often seek to comply with maximal mourning practice. Certainly, more Jewish observance rather than less can help mourners find comfort and consolation. But mourners should be cautious about trying to fulfill every custom conveyed to them by well-meaning friends and relatives as well as by traditional codes of Jewish law. It is easy to be overwhelmed by a sense of obligation and a need to "do the right thing." In a quest for precision, it is possible to miss the opportunity for Jewish tradition to serve the spiritual and emotional needs of mourners.

In this chapter, the words *mitzva* and *mitzvot* are used to refer to the observances of tradition that contemporary Jews should consider seriously as practices for themselves. Jewish tradition focuses on three primary *mitzvot* at the time of death:

Avelut (mourning). This refers to the *obligations/opportunities for mourners* in terms of traditions and customs they observe as part of their mourning. From the rich patterns of observance marking the journey through mourning and back into life, mourners should select those rituals and rites that help support them and lend stability during a time that often appears without structure.

K'vod hamet (the honor and respect due the deceased). This refers to *obligations to the deceased person,* including the care extended to the body between death and burial and the norm of a dignified and respectful interment shortly after death.

Niḥum avelim (comforting the mourners). This refers to the *obligation of friends and family* to support and comfort the mourners. There are rituals and customs pertaining to comforters as well as to those in need of comfort.

For each stage of the journey of mourning, this guide describes *mitzvot* associated with these categories. Discussions of such broader topics as who is a mourner; the Kaddish; cremation; funerals, *shiva* and Jewish holidays; infant death; and suggestions for interfaith and conversionary family circumstances begin on page 173.

Stages of Mourning

Aninut—From Death To Burial.[107] The period from death to burial is one of intense emotion and personal and family disruption. Mourners are involved with making arrangements for the funeral and burial and notifying family and friends.

Mitzvot of Avelut/Mourning. One becomes a mourner upon hearing of a death. The period from when one receives the news of a death up to the burial is called *aninut,* derived from a Hebrew word meaning "impoverished" or "afflicted"—which accurately captures the intensity of the first stage in the journey of mourning.

Aninut is a particularly difficult period. The often shattering news of a loss can be numbing, and yet the inevitable task of beginning to accept the death also claims attention. The necessity of making funeral and burial arrangements often supersedes the need to express the intense and complex emotions that are present.

Upon hearing of the death, mourners recite the *b'raḥa* (benediction), "*Barukh ata Adonay Eloheynu melekh ha-olam, dayan ha-*

emet, Blessed are you, WISE ONE our God, sovereign of all worlds, the true judge."

This ancient benediction reflects our ancestors' belief that all that happens in our world is in some way the will of God, and that therefore even sad news should be acknowledged by affirming God and God's decrees. The traditional words of the Hebrew blessing wrap mourners in the comforting rituals of Judaism. However, those who see God more as a Power operating in and through us than as a Personal Being acting upon us understand this benediction to mean something like "We affirm the blessings of life even as we accept the boundaries of life."

After saying this *b'rakha,* one rends a garment as a sign of grieving. This is called *k'ria* (tearing). A black ribbon often substitutes for an actual garment, and is similarly torn or cut. In many communities this is deferred until the funeral service, but need not be. The garment or ribbon is worn through the end of the *shiva* observance. The tear or the ribbon is on the right side of the chest for all deceased relatives except one's parents, when the tear is on the left, closer to the heart.

During *aninut,* mourners alter their patterns of living in response to the change in their lives brought about by a death, and in anticipation of the observances of *shiva* that commence following the burial. It is customary during *aninut* for mourners to abstain from meat and wine, symbols of enrichment; it is appropriate to withdraw from one's work, both domestic and professional; one avoids entertainment such as movies, shows and concerts.

Jewish tradition urges that burial occur as soon as possible after death. With due time allowed for family notification and necessary travel, funerals normally occur within one to three days following a death; hence the duration of *aninut* is relatively short.

Mitzvot of K'vod Hamet/Honoring the Deceased. Between death and burial, there is great care and concern for the body of the deceased. Arrangements should be made with the funeral director for a *shomer/shomeret* (guardian) to sit with the body so that it is not left alone. A *shomer/shomeret* normally recites from the biblical book of Psalms while in the presence of the body. The origins of this practice may reside in a belief that the body/ soul is vulnerable to supernatural forces following death but before interment. It may also be a survival of ancient pragmatic practices designed to protect the body from animals and insects prior to burial. Today, having a *shomer/shomeret* is recognized as a sign of respect for the deceased.

Families should ascertain that requests by the deceased for organ donation are fulfilled. While Judaism has traditionally restricted organ donation (as well as routine autopsies) as a violation of *k'vod hamet,* liberal Jewish movements affirm that medical benefits to the living outweigh traditional restrictions against organ donation. A small number of contemporary Orthodox authorities have also ruled in favor of organ donation under certain circumstances. Where autopsies advance medical knowledge, families may choose to allow autopsies. (In many communities, local laws often mandate autopsy.)

Tahara (ritual purification and washing of the body) should be arranged. This is normally done by a group of volunteers known as a *ḥevra kadisha,* "sacred society." Today, in addition to a traditional *ḥevra kadisha,* a significant number of Jewish communities have a progressive/liberal *ḥevra kadisha.* Rabbis and/or funeral directors can usually provide the names and contacts for local *ḥevra kadisha* organizations.

Humility and simplicity should guide the burial preparations. Commercial and consumer pressures often conspire at the moment of death, when mourners are most vulnerable and least able to think clearly. A close friend or family member can often help by accompanying mourners to the meeting with the funeral director and gently but firmly communicating the family's preference for traditional rites and rituals. Simple clothes or, according to tradition, humble burial shrouds called *takhrikhim,* are used for interment: in death all are equal. For this same reason, there is a strong preference for a plain wooden casket.

The tendency to overextend on funeral arrangements is often a reflex of a genuine desire to show affection and respect for the deceased. However, ostentation should be avoided. The expenses associated with elaborate arrangements—including fancy caskets and flowers—can be allocated instead to various *tzedaka* (charity) opportunities in memory of the deceased. Prior to the funeral, families should select charities to which donations may be made in memory of the deceased.

Several congregations have created funeral plans that establish the community's preferred and customary rituals to be observed at a time of loss. The arrangements included in such funeral plans are then communicated to any funeral director with whom the family and rabbi may be working.

Mitzvot of Niḥum Avelim/Comforting the Mourners. The normal routines of life are disrupted immediately following a death. Offers to help with shopping, carpooling, picking up relatives arriving from out of town, and similar errands are all appropriate. During *aninut,* family and friends may offer assistance, but visitation is not appropriate prior to the funeral. The family of the deceased is busy with preparations and is not prepared to receive condolences. Jewish tradition teaches that one does not attempt to console mourners prior to the burial.

Halvayat Hamet—The Funeral. Death is a time of isolation for mourners, softened by the presence of family and community. Judaism affirms that in death both the deceased and the mourners are not alone. The next stage in the journey of mourning is *halvayat hamet,* "accompanying the deceased" on his/her journey to the final resting place.

Mitzvot of Avelut/Mourning. If a garment or ribbon has not previously been torn, the *k'ria*/tearing should take place at the funeral service.

In many communities funeral directors seat the mourners in the front row of the chapel, where they receive condolences prior to the funeral service. In other communities the family is ushered into the chapel only when the service is about to begin. Since these are only local customs, mourners should not feel compelled to comply with either model but should choose what feels appropriate and comforting.

Mitzvot of K'vod Hamet/Honoring the Deceased. Funerals can take place anytime except on Shabbat and the first and last days of Jewish holidays. They normally take place during daylight hours.

Jewish tradition mandates that caskets be closed for the funeral service as a sign of respect for the deceased, and to encourage family and friends to remember them as they were in life rather than in death. Viewings and pre-funeral chapel visitations are not in keeping with Jewish tradition.

The funeral-service liturgy is usually brief. Psalms, readings from the Bible, contemporary poems and reflections, and a few specific prayers are included. It is customary (but not obligatory) for a *hesped* (eulogy) to be offered in which the deceased is memorialized. Most often, this will be done by the rabbi, who either will have known the deceased or met with the family to learn about him/her. Sometimes, one or more members of the family may wish to speak briefly at the funeral service. In the interests of not overburdening family and friends with a lengthy service, the rabbi should always be consulted regarding additional speakers at a funeral.

The primary role of mourners at the funeral is to be mourners. Taking on the emotional task of speaking about a loved one during the highly charged time immediately before burial should be carefully considered. As an alternative, a relative or friend might be designated to offer remarks on behalf of the family or to read remarks prepared by one or more of the mourners. Mourners might consider, as an alternative, speaking briefly about the deceased during *shiva* at home, prior to prayer services or prior to recitation of the Kaddish.

Funerals most often take place in funeral parlor chapels, although some communities hold funerals in the synagogue. Graveside funerals, which combine the funeral and burial service, are also common.

When the casket is removed from the chapel, those present stand out of respect. Although local customs vary, in most communities the casket goes first in the procession from the chapel to the hearse and from the hearse to the grave upon reaching the cemetery.

In some communities, pallbearers have the actual responsibility for carrying the casket; elsewhere the role is primarily honorary. Serving as a pallbearer is a custom rather than a law; anyone the family selects as appropriate may serve.

Mitzvot of Niḥum Avelim/Comforting the Mourners. Because funerals often take place close to midday and may involve considerable travel time, mourners may neglect to take care of their nutritional needs and can end up going a long stretch of time without food or drink. Add to this the stress of the death and funeral and any seasonal factors such as extreme heat, and mourners run the risk of weakening themselves or even becoming ill during the day of the funeral.

Those involved in supporting the mourners might prepare packages (sandwiches, snacks, drinks) for the mourners to take along during the ride to/from the funeral home and/or cemetery. Mourners themselves often understandably overlook this and will appreciate the consideration. At the funeral, friends and family provide comfort and consolation primarily by being present. There are few formal opportunities for people to convey condolences. When the funeral and burial are held separately, people will often choose not to continue on to the cemetery after the service. Often, they will seek out the mourners at the conclusion of the service. With the best of intentions of expressing regrets, such interactions when the mourners are in transition from the funeral to the cemetery can be a stressful intrusion. It is preferable to wait until a *shiva* visit to offer condolences.

Halvayat Hamet—The Burial. The funeral is primarily a service of words; the burial is primarily a service of acts. Jewish tradition wisely recognizes the limits of language in confronting this life-boundary moment, and instead directs us to a series of acts with which to bring our loved ones to their final rest.

Mitzvot of *Avelut*/Mourning. The first time that mourners recite the Kaddish prayer is at the cemetery. Again local customs vary: Kaddish may be recited before or after the casket is lowered into the grave.

Where contemporary culture often encourages us to avert our eyes when confronting death, Judaism encourages us to face the reality of mortality. A meaningful tradition is to place two or three spadefuls of earth in the grave. Family members are invited first, followed by any others who wish to do so. While this is often an intense emotional experience, it is also a confirmation and acceptance of the death. Burial is an act of *hesed shel emet* (selfless lovingkindness) on the part of the family and friends. As an act that cannot be reciprocated by the deceased, it highlights the selflessness with which all *mitzvot* may be carried out.

Mourners and comforters are invited to place some earth into the grave after the graveside liturgy is completed. It is the custom to replace the spade or shovel in the mound of earth rather than hand it on to the next person. This may originate in a common belief found in almost all cultures, ancient as well as modern, that death is a contagion. Alternative explanations for retaining this custom might include: each person had a different relationship with the deceased, and so each participates in the burial independently; or, by allowing each person to retrieve and then replace the spade or shovel, we offer individuals the opportunity to fulfill the *mitzva* of *halvayat hamet*.

It is customary to scatter some earth from the Land of Israel into the grave, symbolically linking the life of the deceased to the life of the Jewish people past, present, and future. Funeral directors can usually provide small bags of soil from Israel.

Families are often encouraged to depart from the cemetery as soon as the service is concluded, but it is appropriate to remain at the grave at least until the casket is covered with earth, and preferably until the grave is filled in. However, the circumstances of the death, the emotional and physical condition of the mourners, and weather conditions should be taken into account.

The transition from the cemetery back to the home is poignant and profound. Before leaving the cemetery grounds, some follow the custom of plucking up a few strands of grass and tossing them over the shoulder. Many associate this practice with the biblical verse, "At daybreak [we] are like grass that renews itself . . . by dusk it withers and dries up." (Psalm 90:5–6) or "God remembers that we are but dust" (Psalm 103:14).

Similarly, it is customary to wash one's hands upon leaving the cemetery (or prior to reentering the home—depending on local and family customs). This practice is related to ancient traditions of washing as an act of ritual purification. The acts of plucking grass and washing hands both suggest a common need to demarcate the boundary between death and life—the cemetery and the world outside the cemetery.

Mitzvot of K'vod Hamet/Honoring the Deceased. At the cemetery, the procession normally follows the casket. Tradition suggests that the procession pause several times (seven is the common number) before reaching the grave. Explanations for this custom include a reticence to take final leave of our loved ones, a desire to impress those present with the solemnity of the moment, and an opportunity to reflect on our own mortality.

At graveside, local customs vary: in some places, the casket is lowered before the final prayers are offered; in other locales, the casket remains at ground level until the liturgy is completed.

Jewish law mandates burial in the earth. The process of natural decomposition is considered most gentle and appropriate. Burial in a mausoleum, while not customary in our day, is not prohibited by Jewish tradition and was apparently not uncommon in the early talmudic period. In contemporary Jewish life, cremation is sometimes chosen in place of burial. (For a discussion of cremation, see page 178.)

Mitzvot of **Niḥum Avelim**/Comforting the Mourners. At the cemetery, when the service and the burial are complete and the mourners are preparing to leave, those present customarily form two parallel lines, creating a corridor of comfort for the mourners. It is often difficult to arrange people into this linear configuration without intruding on the emotional intensity of the moment. One way to assist is for the rabbi or other officiant to suggest that after individuals have an opportunity to place earth in the grave, they move into one of two lines leading from the graveside, to be ready to support the mourners on their journey from the cemetery. Those choosing not to place earth can be invited to step into a line as well.

As the mourners pass through, it is customary for those offering comfort to say, "*Hamakom yinaḥem etkhem betokh sha'ar aveley tziyon virushalayim,* May God comfort you along with all the mourners of Zion and Jerusalem." This ancient benediction links the life of each individual Jew to the life of the Jewish people and to the hope for a messianic future. The "mourners of Zion and Jerusalem" will be comforted when, according to traditional Jewish religious myth, the Messiah arrives, Jerusalem is rebuilt and the dead are resurrected. While Reconstructionist Judaism does not affirm a personal messiah or resurrection of the dead, the symbolism of a messianic age of peace and plenitude for all renders this traditional benediction equally appropriate.

Tradition not only recommends but actually requires that the mourners share a meal as a sign of their recommitment to life. It is a *mitzva* of *niḥum avelim*/comforting the mourners for several people to stay behind at the *shiva* home and prepare the traditional *se'udat havra'a*/meal of consolation, so that upon returning from the cemetery, mourners can have some nourishment. Customary foods representing the circle and cycle of life include eggs and lentils. Meat and wine are avoided.

Those preparing the *shiva* home for the return of the mourners should place a basin, pitcher of water and towels outside the door for those who wish to do the customary hand-washing when they return from the cemetery.

Shiva—The First Week.

Shiva ("seven") refers to the traditional period of time following burial that is set aside for mourners to receive condolences and be together. In the biblical tradition, seven is a number of wholeness and completion. The origins of seven days of mourning go back to the earliest generations of the Jewish people, when Joseph mourned his father Jacob (Genesis 50:10).

Mitzvot of Avelut/Mourning. *Shiva* begins when the burial is completed, and regardless of how close to sunset the burial may be, that counts as one day. Since Jewish days begin at sunset, the night of the day of the burial begins the second day of counting for *shiva,* and so forth. If there is a cremation, it is recommended that *shiva* begin from the conclusion of the funeral service prior to, or memorial service subsequent to, the cremation. On Shabbat, public observances of *shiva* are suspended; Kaddish is recited in the synagogue. On Saturday night at sunset, *shiva* observances resume. Shabbat is counted as one of the days of *shiva*.

While *shiva* literally means "seven," in many contemporary Jewish families circumstance and/or choice may result in a decision to reduce the number of days that *shiva* is observed. In order to demonstrate respect for the deceased and to allow mourners a reasonable period in which to be together and share their sadness, it is recommended that the minimum observance consist of not fewer than three days. Jewish law allows those who would be economically harmed to return to work after three days of *shiva*.

In past generations, the family usually observed *shiva* at the home of the deceased. However, any residence that works may be chosen. Mourners are free to sleep at home and come and go from the *shiva* home as necessary, but outside trips (shopping, errands) should be avoided.

With the geographic dispersal of families, people often attend a funeral in a community far from their home. Some people observe part or all of *shiva* in their home communities. Others choose to hold a one-day or one-night additional *shiva* observance when they return home so that local friends and family who may not have been able to travel to the funeral can offer condolences.

At the beginning of *shiva,* upon returning home from the cemetery, a candle that burns for seven days is lit in the *shiva* home. There are differing explanations for this practice; a common one associates light with the soul—"the human soul is the light of God" (Proverbs 20:27). For many mourners, the candle is a symbol of the abiding presence of the memory of the deceased.

During *shiva* mourners refrain from domestic and professional work and generally restrict themselves to the *shiva* home and/or their own home. Mourners abstain from activities identified with recreation and pleasure. They avoid wearing leather shoes and, when seated, customarily sit on low stools or benches, or on chairs or sofas from which the cushions have been removed. Those with physical and/or medical conditions, including pregnancy, which make such seating difficult are exempt.

Cutting hair, shaving, using cosmetics and so forth are avoided during *shiva.* Bathing for hygienic purposes is permissible. Sexual intercourse is avoided insofar as this embodies pleasure and represents (potential) life, both of which are in emotional contrast to death and mourning.

In many *shiva* homes, the custom of covering mirrors is observed. The origins of this practice are likely found in ancient anxieties surrounding death and demons—the concern being that one's image or the soul of the deceased might be imprisoned in a mirror, or that a mirror might be an inadvertent gateway between the realms of life and death. Later Jewish tradition offers two other explanations. One suggests that looking at one's reflection induces vanity, considered inappropriate to the humility that mourning is expected to confer. The other suggests that a mourner who sees her/his bedraggled appearance may be moved to shave or put on make-up in contradiction of Jewish tradition. While no one explanation can substantiate this or any other ritual practice, the emotional power of a tangible disruption of the normal appearance of the home (in ways similar to, for example, removing sofa and chair cushions) is an appropriate expression of the disruption in the family system created by the death.

Prayer services are usually held in the *shiva* home. Since Jews are traditionally enjoined to pray three times daily and mourners do not attend the synagogue during *shiva* (with the exception of Shabbat), it is imperative that they be enabled to pray by bringing the synagogue, as it were, to their home. In many Reconstructionist communities, the custom is to hold services only in the evening, but services may also be held in the morning. If a family chooses not to hold a formal religious service at the home during *shiva,* it is recommended that some structured period of brief Torah study—the reading of part of the weekly Torah portion or other biblical passages, perhaps some of the psalms—be offered instead. Both prayer and study are appropriate as a prelude to the mourners reciting Kaddish.

On the last day, formal mourning practices of *shiva* conclude ("getting up from *shiva*") either following morning prayer services (if they are held) or sometime between early morning and midday. Mourners take a walk around the block or neighborhood as they re-enter life.

Traditional Jewish laws regarding *shiva* and Jewish holidays are complex. For a discussion of *shiva* and Jewish holidays, see page 179.

Mitzvot of K'vod Hamet/Honoring the Deceased. During *shiva,* it is customary to honor the memory of the deceased by telling stories of her/his life and sharing memorabilia, including photographs and video/audio tapes. Many of those coming to offer comfort during *shiva* may not have known the deceased. This is an opportunity to honor her/his memory by recounting something of her/his life.

Mitzvot of Niḥum Avelim/Comforting the Mourners. It is appropriate to visit the *shiva* home to offer condolences and express sympathy for the loss. Sharing memories of the deceased person is also appropriate. Mourners often remember the presence of comforters rather than the words they say. Just sitting with people and providing a sense of solidarity is often enough.

The atmosphere at a *shiva* home should reflect the emotional reality of the family's loss. While serious, it need not always be somber, although solemnity is appropriate when confronting a tragic loss. While all deaths are sad, there are those that come with peace and calm at the end of a long life, and at *shiva* the family may warmly share memories in celebration of the life. Other losses, including sudden and early deaths, accidental deaths, and other shocking tragedies, should be reflected in the tone of the *shiva* home. Friends coming to visit should support the family, recognize their needs and avoid engaging in conversations of a social or business nature that can easily be deferred until outside the *shiva* home.

Helping prepare meals, doing light housekeeping, and volunteering for errands such as shopping and transportation for children are all helpful ways of supporting mourners.

Sh'loshim—The First Month.

The thirty days after the funeral/burial are called *sh'loshim* ("thirty"). For the mourning of all immediate relatives except parents, this period comprises and concludes formal mourning observances. For parents, mourners continue a series of observances for a period of eleven months.

Many contemporary Jews experience losses of other relatives such as a spouse, sibling, or child as equal to (or even greater than) the loss of a parent, and thus choose to continue observing certain mourning practices, especially the recitation of Kaddish beyond *sh'loshim* and even up to the full eleven months normally accorded only for parents.

Mitzvot of Avelut/Mourning.

The first month following death is a period of adjustment during which the intensity of the loss starts to recede as mourners begin to return to the rhythms of their lives. Following the conclusion of *shiva,* mourners can return to their regular professional and domestic work patterns. Mourners no longer sit on low stools, cover mirrors, wear a torn garment/black ribbon, avoid sexual relations, or refrain from shaving.

However, it is customary for mourners to retain some outward observances. During *sh'loshim,* mourners usually avoid parties, celebrations, and public entertainment. One can attend bar/bat mitzvah services, weddings and other lifecycle events but may choose not to attend the celebrations often attached to those rituals. It is customary to avoid wearing new clothing during *sh'loshim.* Mourners continue to recite Kaddish during this period.

Mitzvot of K'vod Hamet/Honoring the Deceased. The settling of the estate of the deceased, closing of her/his residence, and disposition of her/his property often occur during *sh'loshim.* While often emotionally difficult for mourners, these necessary activities are part of the process of accepting and working through the loss.

When we invoke the name of a person who is deceased, it is customary to add *"alav hashalom"* (for a male) or *"aleha hashalom"* (for a female) ("peace be upon him/her") after the name. Another phrase often used is *"zikhrono livrakha"* (for a male) or *"zikhrona livrakha"* (for a female) ("his/her memory is a blessing").

It is customary to conclude *sh'loshim* with a gathering of friends and family in which words of Torah are exchanged and studied in honor of the deceased.

Mitzvot of Niḥum Avelim/Comforting the Mourners. After the funeral and *shiva,* as visitations end, mourners are often unintentionally abandoned. While free to resume their normal home and work lives, mourners may still want or need support and assistance. Phone calls, letters and brief visits may all be appropriate and appreciated. Invitations for Shabbat and/or holiday meals may help. Offering to attend synagogue with mourners, especially those who are alone, can help avoid the isolation that often settles on surviving spouses. In general, friends should check in with mourners during *sh'loshim* to see if they are all right and if they need anything.

Yahrtzeit—The First Year.
The journey of mourning is not always level. As the days and weeks from the death increase, there is often a discernible diminishment in the intensity of grieving. But at significant moments in the year, such as birth-

days, holidays and anniversaries, mourners may find themselves revisiting their loss as if it were only yesterday.

Mitzvot of Avelut/Mourning. When mourning for a parent, certain practices extend beyond the thirty days of *sh'loshim* for a total of eleven months. Most common is the recitation of Kaddish, followed by avoidance of public celebrations and entertainment. When mourners choose to extend mourning beyond *sh'loshim* for other relatives, these practices may similarly be extended.

Traditional explanations for the tradition of eleven months of mourning derive from certain rabbinic legends that associate the year following death as a period of purging of the soul of the deceased in anticipation of the soul's return to God. These legends associate the recitation of Kaddish during that time as aiding the cleansing of the soul. To avoid implying that the soul of the deceased was so severely tainted as to require a full year of mourning, the tradition became to conclude formal mourning practices after eleven months. A historical perspective would suggest that the eleven-month period preceded any attempts to explain its origins. Once the practice became standard, attempts were made to explain a custom that had already attained communal consensus.

An alternative explanation may be found in the analogy to *shiva* ending on the morning of the seventh day rather than at sunset. As the first year following the death comes near to its conclusion, we abridge the fullness of twelve months and conclude instead just as the last month of the first year is beginning. In so doing, we glimpse the Jewish affirmation of life over death. Before the first anniversary of the loss, we give ourselves a full month to resume our entire routine of activities with none of the restrictions of mourning. When we do in fact reach that anniversary, we come to it with life renewed, rather than as mourners.

The first anniversary of the loss is the first observance of the *yahrtzeit*. A Yiddish word meaning "year's time," *yahrtzeit* corresponds to the anniversary date of the death, reckoned according to the Jewish calendar date of death (not burial). Since Jewish days start at sunset, calculating the *yahrtzeit* date requires knowing if the death occurred before or after nightfall. If after, the date for the *yahrtzeit* will be the next day on the Jewish calendar. Rabbis can assist in determining the Jewish date of the *yahrtzeit* if the family knows the date on the civil calendar and the time of death.

The first *yahrtzeit* has a unique significance. Mourners inevitably invoke memories of the day of their loss; the presence of their loved one may feel more tangible; memories may be intensely present, and there can be a recurrence of feelings of grief and sadness that have dissipated during the year.

The practices associated with *yahrtzeit* are customarily observed by those who were the mourners. Other family members, such as grandchildren, may also choose to observe a *yahrtzeit*. When those obligated to mourning have themselves deceased, others in the family may choose to assure that the *yahrtzeit* will continue to be observed.

A memorial candle is kindled in the home the evening preceding the date of the *yahrtzeit*. While Jewish tradition does not provide a specific liturgy, contemporary Jews have created a number of meditations, prayers and blessings. Personal reflections, a poem, reading or song are all appropriate as well. A Reconstructionist version can be found in the home prayer book *Kol Haneshamah: Shirim Uverahot, Songs, Blessings and Rituals For the Home*, page 136.

Yahrtzeits are also marked by the recitation of Kaddish. Traditionally this is done on the actual *yahrtzeit* day if mourners can attend a daily worship service for any or all of the three customary daily prayer services. In many communities, *yahrtzeits* are announced at Shabbat services, and those observing *yahrtzeit* any time within seven days recite Kaddish. Local customs vary regarding Shabbat observances coming either before or after the *yahrtzeit* date. Check with the rabbi/congregation as to the practices in a given community. Many communities follow the custom of offering those observing *yahrtzeit* an *aliya* (recitation of blessings over the reading of the Torah) and/or designating one of the *aliyot*/Torah-reading sections for anyone observing a *yahrtzeit* that week.

It is customary to make contributions to *tzedaka* and/or to engage in learning/teaching of Torah on a *yahrtzeit* in honor of the memory of the deceased. The *yahrtzeit* continues to be observed each year on the anniversary date.

Mitzvot of K'vod Hamet/Honoring the Deceased. Families normally arrange for a headstone, monument or marker to be inscribed, erected and dedicated at the burial site. Monuments usually carry the English and Hebrew names of the deceased as well as the English and Hebrew dates of birth and death. Families may choose a brief additional inscription.

Since headstone dedications are in the realm of custom and not law, considerable latitude can be taken in deciding when to erect a monument. Mourners do need time to adjust to their loss. A dedication that occurs in close proximity to the funeral (anytime from *sh'loshim* to approximately six months following the loss) will often carry so much of the emotional echo of the funeral as to make it feel like a second round of grieving. It is recommended that dedications take place sometime in the second half of the year following a death. Seasonal and climatic factors can and should be taken into account.

Family events, whether informal or formal, often bring family members together and provide an opportunity for a dedication. For example, in today's Jewish community, the Friday preceding or Sunday following a bar or bat mitzvah ceremony is increasingly used for dedications. Individuals and families should assess the emotional impact on families (and especially on bar and bat mitzvah students) of holding a dedication in proximity to a family celebration.

There is little formal liturgy associated with dedications. It is customary to recite the memorial prayer *El Maley Raḥamim* ("God full of compassion") in Hebrew and/or English, as well as Kaddish. Additional psalms, readings, poems and/or family reflections can be shared as well.

Mitzvot of Niḥum Avelim/Comforting the Mourners. Friends should stay in touch with mourners during the year after a loss. While there may be a decreasing need for specific support, the constancy of friendship is important. Widows and widowers often report that in the year following the loss of their partner/spouse, they experienced the loss of friendships with couples who may not have known how to adjust. Friends can also intervene if they notice an absence of adjustment to the loss, and may be able to suggest some form of counseling.

Hazkarat Neshamot—The Memorializing of Souls.

Beginning after the conclusion of the first *yahrtzeit,* the *Yizkor* (memorial) service is recited in memory of deceased relatives on the holidays of Pesaḥ, Sukkot-Shemini Atzeret, Shavuot and Yom Kippur. During the *Yizkor* service recited in the synagogue, the privacy of loss is shared with the community; we join with all who have taken the journey of mourning, those who have experienced recent losses and those who memorialize relatives who are long gone. Invisible presences join us as memories are invoked, names remembered and prayers offered.

On the holidays when *Yizkor* is recited, it is customary to light a memorial *(yahrtzeit)* candle in the home in the evening as the holiday begins, prior to kindling the festival candles.

Betz'ror Haḥayim—The Bond of Life. Jewish tradition is remarkably diverse in its perspectives on what happens after death. As an evolving religious tradition, Judaism has passed through several stages in its thinking about the afterlife. In the biblical period, life was understood as primarily this-worldly, and whatever afterlife may have been envisioned was vaguely understood as a shadowy and ethereal semi-existence in a place called Sheol. Some biblical texts identify Gehinom as a place where punishment is meted out after death. While certain of the psalms and one evocative passage in the book of the prophet Ezekiel seem to suggest a belief in resurrection, the testimony of the biblical writers suggests that the death of the individual was seen as final, and that eternality was understood to be in the ongoing life of the Jewish people.

With the rise of the rabbinic period beginning two centuries before the Common Era, a more focused concern on the fate of the individual emerged. Evidence from this period in late scripture (the book of Daniel) and in early forms of Jewish liturgy points to an emerging belief in *teḥiyat hametim*/resurrection of the dead and *olam haba*/the [heavenly] world to come. Other teachers and authorities affirmed the eternality of the soul while denying the resurrection of the body. Some medieval forms of Jewish mysticism, as well as some forms of contemporary Hasidism, support belief in *gilgul nefashot*/reincarnation.

From the rabbinic period until the advent of modernity, whatever individual Jews may have believed about life after death —bodily resurrection, a heavenly world to come, eternal souls, or reincarnation, as well as any number of variants on these themes—classical Jewish liturgy affirmed that God was *"mehayey hametim,"* the "One who revives the dead."

With the rise of modernity, the belief in bodily resurrection and a heavenly realm receded before science, reason and rationality. The early Reform and the later Reconstructionist prayer books eliminated references to resurrection and the world to come. The language of the current Reconstructionist liturgy affirms that God is *"mehayey kol hay,"* the "Fount of Life, who gives and renews life."

Reconstructionist Judaism, following the insights of its founder Mordecai M. Kaplan, sees the current period in Jewish life as a this-worldly period, in contrast to the rabbinic and medieval periods of Judaism, which were other-worldly in their emphasis. While no longer affirming many of the traditional ideas about life beyond death, Reconstructionist Judaism recognizes that eternality and immortality remain important spiritual concepts that can be understood from naturalistic and humanistic perspectives.

Like our biblical ancestors, we affirm faith in the eternality of the Jewish people. Our journey through life as Jews contributes to the totality of what the Jewish people have been and will become. Through our commitments and contributions, we can leave a legacy that strengthens and supports the Torah tradition as it is handed on to succeeding generations. And like our rabbinic ancestors, we affirm that beyond the limits of human life and the human body are our individual *neshamot*/souls with which we are graced and for which we are responsible. At death, the body comes to rest, but the soul returns to God.

Some contemporary Jews believe that the soul literally survives, cared for by a God capable of calling life itself into being, and capable of preserving it beyond its earthly journey. For others, immortality is conferred through memory, as the values we lived by and the contributions we made to family, friends and the world are honored by those who live on after us. Some understand each soul to be like a wave, drawn back into the ocean from which it was essentially never separate. A smaller number no doubt find comfort and meaning in the more traditional ideas of a world to come, where the injustices of this world are made right and the peace for which we long is finally bestowed.

Jewish life today is as diverse as it has been in any of the preceding three millennia. While religious movements in Judaism may affirm or alter traditional ideas, individual Jews will choose what they believe about life beyond death—regardless of their denominational affiliation. In such a highly personal area of spiritual conviction, that is entirely appropriate. There is a wonderful diversity of Jewish views on life beyond death, and a remarkable humility in Judaism which affirms that in ways we can never quite know—and perhaps do not need to know—the sacredness of human life transcends and survives beyond death.

Issues Relating to Mourning

Who Is A Mourner? Jewish tradition defines mourners as anyone having a first-degree relationship to the deceased: parents, spouses, children, and siblings. While sadness and grieving extend throughout a family system, only those in primary relationships to the deceased are, from the perspective of Jewish tradition, *obligated* to ritual observances of mourning.

So while grandchildren grieve the loss of grandparents, the grandchildren are not *obligated,* for example, to observe *shiva* or recite Kaddish—although as participants in the family system at a time of loss, they obviously partake of the atmosphere of sadness. Similarly, in-laws may experience a sense of loss, but are not obligated as mourners.

Family members who are not *obligated* as mourners often *voluntarily* assume some of the obligations of mourning. In cases where, for example, no one is left to mourn or say Kaddish for a certain relative—or if no one else in the family shares the Jewish commitments that would support such observance—another relative might take on the *mitzvot* of mourning and Kaddish for that deceased relative. Another example might be a grandchild who is exceptionally close to a deceased grandparent, and who out of affection chooses to offer Kaddish for her/him during the period after death. There is nothing wrong with voluntarily taking on certain observances that are not required.

Kaddish. The Kaddish prayer originated in the days of the Talmud (c. 100–500 C.E.). The earliest form, the *Kaddish Derabanan* ("The Kaddish over study"), was originally offered to conclude a period of Torah learning; it had no connection with death and mourning. Over the generations, several versions of the Kaddish developed. Some versions, such as the *Ḥatzi Kaddish* (abridged Kaddish) and the *Kaddish Shalem* (expanded Kaddish), appear in synagogue liturgy as punctuation points between sections of the services.

The *Kaddish Yatom,* or Mourner's Kaddish that we associate with mourning observances, gradually emerged in the Middle Ages. In addition to recitation at the burial and during the subsequent mourning period, today Kaddish is also recited on a *yahrtzeit* (anniversary of a death) and at *Yizkor* (synagogue memorial service held on Pesaḥ, Shavuot, Sukkot-Shemini Atzeret and Yom Kippur).

There is one version, known as the burial Kaddish, that in fact makes reference to death, but it is rarely recited. The Kaddish with which most Jews are familiar does not mention death at all, but is rather an affirmation of the Godliness that inheres in life itself despite the boundaries of life. It is an affirmation that while a life has come to an end, life itself continues on with all its possibilities for the future. Perhaps that is why the prevailing theme of Kaddish is the hope for the coming of a world governed by Godliness.

Who recites Kaddish? Keeping in mind how Jewish tradition differentiates between those *obligated* as mourners and those who may *voluntarily choose* to adopt some or all of the requirements of mourning, Kaddish is traditionally understood as an obligation only of immediate first-degree family members—the same people who are obligated to observe *shiva*. While some Jews have retained the folk practice of engaging someone to recite the Kaddish on behalf of their deceased, Reconstructionist Judaism expects mourners themselves to take responsibility for this *mitzva*.

In many communities, it has become the custom in synagogue services for everyone to recite the Kaddish. While many Jews find this solidarity to be a source of comfort, there is a case to be made for allowing the mourners to recite the Kaddish alone, especially at the burial and perhaps during *shiva* as well. It is their first formal act of mourning, inaugurating the *shiva;* it is a time when they do truly stand apart from everyone else because of their relationship to the deceased; it is an affirmation among them of what binds them as a family. Kaddish is not a prayer intended for all people in general but for individual people in particular.

How long does one recite Kaddish? Jewish tradition wisely demarcates an outside boundary for formal mourning, suggesting that while grieving is both necessary and appropriate, re-entering life after loss is also important. Tradition says that for a parent, one recites Kaddish for eleven months, counting from the day of the burial. For all other relatives for whom one is obligated to mourn, Kaddish is to be recited for thirty days, again counting from the burial. Many Jews find it appropriate to recite Kaddish beyond thirty days for non-parent relatives. While there is no obligation to do so, one certainly may do so if it provides comfort and helps on the journey through mourning. The outside boundary for regular recitation of Kaddish as a mourner is eleven months. Long-term memorialization of loved ones should be found in acts undertaken in their name and memory.

Kaddish Without a Minyan. Kaddish is among the prayers that traditionally require a *minyan* (prayer quorum of ten adult Jews) for recitation. One reason that comforters assemble at a *shiva* home is to allow mourners to recite Kaddish as part of prayer services.

In light of contemporary needs and people's work and family schedules, it is often difficult for mourners to attend a scheduled service at a synagogue in order to recite Kaddish following *shiva*. The question arises as to whether an individual might recite Kaddish at home, in the absence of a *minyan,* on a private basis if s/he cannot attend synagogue to do so.

Mourners during their period of formal mourning share a solidarity that is most tangible when they join with other mourners in reciting Kaddish in congregational services. Many mourners testify to the comfort provided by regular (if not always daily) attendance at services, even if prior to the death in their family they did not regularly attend synagogue. In many ways, the often extra effort necessary to fit synagogue attendance into one's schedule is rewarded by a sense of calm, by new friendships made, and by an awareness that even in a period of need one also contributes to a community that relies on people showing up for each other.

However, in light of personal, professional, partnering and parenting schedules, it is difficult for many people to maintain even the best-intentioned commitments towards daily synagogue attendance. Additionally, it is a reality of the contemporary Jewish community that many congregations do not schedule daily services, forcing people to attend services in a congregation other than their own. Individual recitation of Kaddish, even in the absence of a *minyan,* does help maintain a pattern of ritual and regularity that is part of the journey of mourning. While joining with a community for prayer is optimal, if mourners cannot manage daily synagogue attendance and/or their congregation does not provide for daily prayer services, then Kaddish can be recited at home. Since congregations do hold services on Shabbat, mourners should make every effort to join their communities on Shabbat evening and/or Shabbat morning to recite Kaddish within the community.

Since Kaddish originated as a prayer marking the conclusion of a period of Torah study, it is also appropriate, either in addition to or perhaps in place of the recitation of Kaddish (depending on individual comfort levels), for mourners to set aside a few minutes each day for some form of Torah study. In addition to the weekly Torah portion or biblical texts such as the Psalms, mourners might consult any number of publications that comprise Jewish "thoughts for a day," some of which are specifically written for the observance of a period of mourning.

Cremation. Cremation is a complex issue. Jewish law is un-equivocal in prohibiting cremation: burial in the earth is the norm. The earliest chapters of the Torah are invoked in support of this practice. The name *Adam* derives from the noun *adama* (earthling/human), and the Torah teaches that "dust you are and to dust you shall return" (Genesis 3:10). The Jewish belief in bodily resurrection, which was common until the advent of modernity, also likely influenced the prohibition against cremation.

While many liberal Jews do not affirm resurrection of the body, other contemporary concerns inform discussions regarding cremation. Prominent among them is the evocative agony of the Holocaust. Jews living in the post-Holocaust era cannot escape the association of cremation with the annihilation of European Jewry during the Second World War. For many Jews, this in itself is enough to negate cremation as a choice.

From the perspective of the needs of the mourners, cremation negates the possibilities of many Jewish rituals of mourning and memorializing—such as the burial service itself, the placing of a headstone, and having a place to visit for surviving family. Cremation may not provide the sense of closure that a burial often does.

In a pluralistic Jewish community, however, some Jews will choose cremation over burial. Some raise concerns about ceme-teries in terms of environmental issues and use of scarce natural resources. Others may cite concerns about the costs associated with burial in contrast to cremation (although it is important to contrast the actual costs for a traditional Jewish burial that would minimize extravagance and unnecessary additions such as flowers). Yet others choose cremation for spiritual or religious reasons as they understand them.

It is important for the family members to discuss such choices early on. Confronting cremation directives after death can cause conflict and heartache for the family if there is disagreement. A conflict of values may arise. An adult child opposed to cremation may wonder how to respect a parent's decision for cremation. Siblings or spouses may disagree about whether to support a decision for cremation.

Families in which an individual is considering cremation should discuss and attempt to resolve any differences well in advance of being confronted with the actual death. Adult children often feel obligated to honor the wishes of their parent/s even if the directives they leave indicate practices contrary to Jewish tradition and/or the comfort of the children. In navigating this sensitive area, some people will feel that the *mitzva* of *kibud av v'em*/honoring one's parents is determinative. Others will want to note that Judaism does not require children to carry out directives that are contrary to Jewish law, even if that was the desire of their parent/s. Different families will arrive at different decisions. Whatever decision is reached, families should strive to maintain *k'vod hamet*/respect for the deceased.

It is important to consult with one's rabbi to ascertain her/his position on cremation and officiation, and to identify policies and customs of the local community. Rabbis can also clarify issues and help families discuss the issues they need to resolve.

When there is to be a cremation, it is recommended that a funeral service be conducted prior to the disposition of the body rather than following the cremation. Local customs vary, but ashes may be buried in many Jewish cemeteries.

Jewish Holidays and *Shiva*. According to Jewish law, *shiva* is ended, regardless of how many days have been observed, when a minimum of one hour has been observed before one of the major holidays begins. These include Rosh Hashanah and Yom Kippur, Pesaḥ, Sukkot, and Shavuot.

When a death and burial occur after a holiday has commenced but while it is still being observed (for example, the third day of Pesaḥ), the *shiva* is supposed to be delayed until after the holiday concludes.

These practices suggest that the observances shared by all Jews (holidays) supersede those that are restricted to some Jews (in this case, mourners). They also speak to a practical reality, namely that those who might be expected to come as comforters would, in a traditional community, be involved in the observance of the holidays and unlikely to be available to provide the very support that mourners might need.

For many contemporary Jews, however, the inability to observe *shiva* fully because of the intervention of a holiday is experienced as a lost opportunity. Unable to shift between the sadness of mourning and the celebration of the holiday, many Jews are left with an incomplete experience on both counts.

It is difficult to disregard traditional teachings. The Jewish holidays are powerful; we feel the pull of community even in our moments of individual sorrow. Few Jews could imagine forgoing the Pesaḥ Seder or Kol Nidre night in order to observe *shiva*. But it is also difficult to disregard the emotional realities of a family following a death.

It is advisable to consult with a rabbi about the appropriate accommodation of *shiva* to holidays in light of personal, family and community circumstances and of customs and values. From a liberal perspective balancing the imperatives and precedents of tradition with contemporary needs, the following adaptations may be considered:

- If *shiva* is already being observed when Rosh Hashanah, Yom Kippur or Shavuot begins, rather than cutting off the remainder of *shiva,* the formal/public aspects of *shiva* should cease (as on Shabbat) until the holiday is concluded. A full or modified continuation of *shiva* observance might resume at that time, with the intervening holiday days being counted (as is Shabbat) as part of the seven days.

- If *shiva* is already being observed when Pesaḥ and Sukkot commence, public observances of *shiva* should be suspended on the first and last days (which are "full" holiday observances), but intermediate days *(Ḥol Hamo'ed)* should count toward the days of *shiva* and may be observed as a full or modified continuation of *shiva.*

- Funerals traditionally do not occur on full holiday days. A funeral may occur during intermediate days *(Ḥol Hamo'ed)* of Pesaḥ or Sukkot as well as on Purim or Ḥanuka. When that happens, rather than waiting until after the holiday, *shiva* might begin from the burial and continue until the onset of the closing day of the holiday, when it would either conclude or be suspended until the holiday ends, depending on the counting of *shiva* days.

- Festivals normally affect the counting of the thirty days for *sh'loshim* as well, with the general tendency being for the onset of holidays to abridge or conclude the *sh'loshim* even if thirty days have not elapsed. Since the function of *sh'loshim* is to carry mourners through the first month of the loss, it is suggested that *sh'loshim* be counted as thirty days from the funeral regardless of the intervention of holidays.

Infant Death. In Jewish law, the full requirements of mourning only apply when the deceased has lived beyond thirty days.

While from a contemporary perspective this may appear harsh, in pre-modern times, when small communities had a high incidence of infant mortality, this was intended to be a compassionate gesture that would relieve individuals and the community from what would have been an almost continuous cycle of *shiva* and mourning.

Today, however, it is important to affirm that (with the agreement of the family) in the tragic cases of infant death, the rituals of Jewish mourning should be available to the family so that, in consultation with a rabbi, they can select the observances that would be comforting. While mourning a life of but a few hours, days or weeks is different than mourning a life lived over a period of many years, the sense of loss and grief experienced by the family deserves both respect and response from the Jewish community and Jewish tradition.

Interfaith Issues. In view of the changing demography of the Jewish community, with increasing numbers of intermarried and conversionary families welcomed into our congregations, a series of questions arises regarding mourning practices. In view of the complex and highly personal nature of these issues as they occur in individual families, it is helpful to consult with a rabbi when making decisions about observances of mourning. While the evolution of community customs and norms in this area is still very much in process, the following guidelines reflect an emerging sense of how to respond sensitively to interfaith issues of Jewish rituals for mourning.

Mourning for Non-Jews. The question of whether Jews are obligated to observe mourning practices for non-Jews has received consideration in traditional Jewish sources primarily regarding the obligations that converts to Judaism have to mourn the death of their (non-Jewish) parents (and by extension, other first-degree relatives). The majority of opinions indicate that while a convert to Judaism has no obligation to observe traditional Jewish mourning practices, including the recitation of Kaddish, for her/his parents, the convert may certainly do so if s/he wishes. A minority perspective suggests that such observance might be mandatory rather than optional.

It can be deduced from this reasoning that a Jewish spouse might not be obligated to observe traditional mourning practices for a non-Jewish partner, but would certainly not be prohibited from doing so.

The assumptions behind this reasoning are not necessarily shared by contemporary Jews. Whereas traditional Jewish law focused on the *religious identity of the deceased,* liberal Jews would more likely focus on the *emotional and spiritual needs of the surviving family members.* The resources of Jewish tradition should help Jews throughout the period of loss and mourning. When the non-Jewish spouse/partner in an interfaith marriage dies, it is entirely appropriate for the surviving Jewish spouse/partner to observe the rituals of mourning. For these reasons, converts are encouraged to observe Jewish mourning practices for their non-Jewish relatives.

Non-Jews as Mourners. When a non-Jewish spouse/partner experiences the death of a Jewish spouse, the circumstances can be more complex. The non-Jewish spouse/partner may want a high degree of involvement with Jewish ritual, or, conversely, may not want to be under the presumption of participating in specifically Jewish observances.

The degree to which a non-Jew chooses to participate in Jewish rituals of mourning will vary. If the non-Jewish spouse/partner is an active and/or affirming member of another religious community, s/he presumably participates in the rituals and traditions of that faith community as they pertain to and help support mourners, and will look primarily to that community at a time of loss.

When the non-Jewish spouse/partner is not active in or affirming of another religious tradition, the synagogue may in fact be his/her sole religious community, notwithstanding that s/he has never converted to Judaism. A community should show support for this member as it would for any other member. There may be adaptations and/or modifications of Jewish mourning practices. For example, at a *shiva* observance there may or may not be a recitation of the Jewish evening prayers; if there is, the surviving spouse may or may not recite Kaddish, but the Jewish members of the congregation present should do so as a way for the community to mourn the loss.

Non-Jews are not obligated to observe *mitzvot*. They need not take on specifically Jewish observances, such as *k'ria* and reciting Kaddish. However, consider the example of a family with a Jewish father, non-Jewish mother and Jewish children. If the husband dies and the children (and other Jewish family members) are observing rituals of mourning while the wife is not, she would perhaps rightly feel excluded at a significant emotional moment in the life of the family. From that perspective, wearing a torn garment or a *k'ria* ribbon and joining in the recitation of the Kaddish might be appropriate.

In general, non-Jews in Reconstructionist communities would be encouraged to share in the rituals of mourning that are in the realm of custom (as examples: placing earth in a grave, washing hands on returning from the cemetery, sitting on low stools during *shiva*), while considering the appropriateness of sharing rituals that specifically presume Jewish identity (as examples: reciting Kaddish or the benediction for the *k'ria*).

Conclusion

The Bible teaches:

> For everything there is a season,
> a time for every experience under heaven.
> A time to be born and a time to die;
> a time to weep and a time to laugh;
> A time to grieve and a time to dance;
> a time to seek and a time to lose;
> A time to keep and a time to let go;
> a time to tear and a time to mend.
>
> Ecclesiastes, Chapter 3

Each generation, given the gift of life by those who came before, must eventually confront the loss of life. Mortality is the common condition of humanity, transcending religions, cultures and nations. Our human relationships give us warmth, meaning, companionship and love. And when those relationships are severed by death, we are, appropriately, plunged into despair and grief.

Before we can let go of those we have loved, we pause. We pause in order to take note of a life that has come to its end. We pause to acknowledge grief, and we pause long enough to allow those who grieve to be surrounded by those who love them. And we pause because whenever parting comes, it comes too soon, and we do not want to have to say goodbye.

We look for the strength to withstand the sadness of loss and for the courage to endure in the presence of death. We pray for the ability to give as well as to receive comfort in our moments of mourning. We search for light amidst the darkness, striving to accept the blessing of life itself, which death so often seeks to deny. Judaism celebrates life as a blessing and a gift, and occasions of loss can make us aware—as perhaps no other occasions can—of the need to cherish each moment of life that we are given.

As Jews, we face the common human moment of grieving as other Jews have faced it before us, strengthened by a Power that bestows life and redeems us from death, comforted by the symbols and traditions of our people and by the friends and family who sit with us and reassure us with their presence. In our inevitable moments of loss, may we be granted the peace that comes with the passing of time and the sustaining power of love that never dies. And may we so lead our lives that when the time comes for others to memorialize us, they will do so with affection, respect and love.

ABOUT THE AUTHORS

DR. ELLIOT N. DORFF is Rector and Distinguished Professor of Philosophy at the University of Judaism in Los Angeles and Vice Chair of the Conservative movement's Committee on Jewish Law and Standards. Currently a member of the federal National Human Resources Protections Advisory Panel, he has served on several other federal government commissions on health-care. He completed studies for the rabbinate at the Jewish Theological Seminary and earned his Ph.D. from Columbia University.

RABBI AMY EILBERG is a co-founder of the Bay Area Jewish Healing Center, where she directed the Center's Jewish Hospice Care Program. Nationally known as a leader of the Jewish heal-

ing movement, she teaches and writes on issues of Jewish spiritu-
ality and healing. She currently serves as a pastoral counselor in
private practice in Palo Alto, California. She studied for the
rabbinate at the Jewish Theological Seminary.

RABBI RICHARD HIRSH is Executive Director of the Reconstructionist Rabbinical Association and an Adjunct Instructor at the
Reconstructionist Rabbinical College (RRC). He is Editor of
The Reconstructionist, a journal of contemporary thought and
practice. He studied for the rabbinate at RRC.

DR. WILLIAM KAVESH is Director of Geriatric Primary Care at
the Philadelphia Veterans Affairs Medical Center and Clinical
Assistant Professor of Medicine at the University of Pennsylvania
School of Medicine. He earned his M.D. at the Albert Einstein
School of Medicine and a Masters in Public Health at the Harvard
University School of Health.

RABBI MYRIAM KLOTZ is the former Director of the Kimmel-
Spiller Jewish Healing Center of Jewish Family Services in Wil-
mington, Delaware. The founder and director of the Miriam's
Well Jewish Healing Rabbinic Internship program, she also serves
as a spiritual director at the Reconstructionist Rabbinical College.
She writes and speaks nationally on Jewish healing. She earned
her Master of Arts in Hebrew Literature at RRC, where she
became a rabbi.

CHAPLAIN SHEILA SEGAL is Pastoral Care Supervisor for the
Philadelphia Geriatric Center and Co-Director of Yedid Nefesh,
the Jewish Hospice Program of the Delaware Valley. A certified
Jewish chaplain, she was Editor-in-Chief of the Jewish Publication

Society. She wrote *Women of Valor: Stories of Great Jewish Women Who Helped Shape the Twentieth Century.*

RABBI DAVID TEUTSCH is President of the Reconstructionist Rabbinical College, where he also serves as Myra and Louis Wiener Professor of Contemporary Jewish Civilization and Director of the Center for Jewish Ethics. He earned his Ph.D. in Organizational Ethics at the Wharton School, and his Master of Arts and Master of Hebrew Literature at Hebrew Union College in New York.

DR. PAUL ROOT WOLPE is a faculty associate of the Center for Bio-Ethics and Assistant Professor of Psychiatry and of Sociology at the University of Pennsylvania, where he is also Director of the Program in Psychiatry and Ethics. He is Chief of Bio-Ethics for NASA and Senior Fellow of the Leonard Davis Institute for Health Economics. He earned his Ph.D. in Medical Sociology from Yale University.

NOTES

1. B. Sanhedrin 91a–91b. See also Mekhilta, Beshalaḥ, Shira, ch. 2 (edited by Horowitz-Rabin, 1960, p. 125); Leviticus Raba 4:5; Yalkut Shimoni on Leviticus 4:2 (464); Tanḥuma, Vayikra 6. The very development of the term *neshama* from meaning physical breath to one's inner being bespeaks Judaism's view that the physical and the spiritual are integrated.

2. M. Pe'ah 1:1; B. Kiddushin 40b.

3. M. Avot.

4. B. Berakhot 17a; the earlier rabbinic teaching cited at the end as what we have learned appears in B. *Menaḥot* 110a. While a few of the classical rabbis belonged to wealthy families, most were menial laborers and studied when they could. Hillel, for example, was so poor that he became the symbol of the poor man who nevertheless found the time and money to study Torah (B. Yoma 35b); Akiba had been a shepherd before he devoted himself to study at age 40, subsisting on the price he received for the bundle of wood he collected each day (Avot d'Rabbi

Natan, ch. 6); Joshua was a charcoal burner (B. Berakhot 28a); Yose bar Halafta worked in leather (B. Shabbat 49b); Yohanan was a sandal maker (M. Avot 4:14); Judah was a baker (J. Haggiga 77b); and Abba Saul kneaded dough (B. Pesaḥim 34a) and had been a grave digger (B. Nidah 24b).

5. Elliot N. Dorff, *Matters of Life and Death: A Jewish Approach to Modern Medical Ethics* (Philadelphia: Jewish Publication Society, 1998), pp. 395–423.

6. Leviticus Raba 34:3.

7. Address, Y. H. Kahn, "On Choosing the Hour of Our Death," in Address & James, *Voluntary Active Euthanasia-Assisted Suicide* (Philadelphia: UAHC, 1993), p. 25.

8. Mishneh Torah, Hilkhot Deot 4.1.

9. Kiddushin 66a.

10. Pirkei Avot 5:24.

11. See, for example, J. D. Bleich, "Treatment of the Terminally Ill," in *Tradition* 30(3), pp. 51–87.

12. See Richard Address, "Redefining the Dialogue on Voluntary Euthanasia" in Address & James, *op. cit.* and A. James Rudin, Testimony before the House Committee on Environment Subcommittee on Health and Environment, March 6, 1997.

13. President's Commission for the Study of Ethical Problems in Medicine and Biomedical and Behavioral Research, *Making Healthcare Decisions* (Washington, D.C.: U.S. Government Printing Office, 1982).

14. William N. Kavesh, "Self-Determination and Long-Term Care" in M. B. Kapp, ed., *Patient Self-Determination in Long-Term Care* (New York: Springer, 1982).

15. "Patient Self-Determination Act State Law Guide," American Bar Association, Washington, D.C., 1991.

16. Yalkut, Hukkat §764.

17. B. Nedarim 40a.

18. Benjamin Freedman, *Duty and Healing, Foundations of a Jewish Bioethics* (New York: Routledge, 1999).

19. Midrash Shir Hashirim 2:35.

20. Leo Baeck, *The Essence of Judaism* (New York: Shocken Books, 1948), pp. 211–12.

21. Elisabeth Kübler-Ross, *On Death and Dying* (New York: Macmillan Publishing Co., 1969).

22. See Joanne Lynn and Joan Harrold, *Handbook for Mortals: Guidance for People Facing Serious Illness* (New York: Oxford University Press, 1999) for a wonderful section on communication with the dying. The book is a marvelous resource in general for those dying, or caring for a dying loved one.

23. In Elie Wiesel, *Somewhere A Master* (New York: Summit Books, 1982), p. 94.

24. Bernard Siegel, *Love, Medicine, and Miracles* (New York: Harper-Collins, 1987).

25. Exodus 15:25.

26. Kings 4:34.

27. W. N. Kavesh, "Jews and Disease: Ancient Cures and Remedies" in Siegel & Rheins, *The Jewish Almanac* (New York: Bantam, 1980).

28. A. Green, *Tormented Master: A Life of Rabbi Nahman of Bratslav* (University of Alabama Press, 1979), p. 243.

29. T. Shire, *Hebrew Magic Amulets* (New York: Behrman House, 1979), pp. 13–14.

30. See W. N. Kavesh, "Jewish Medical Ethics" in Siegel, Strassfeld & Strassfeld, *The Second Jewish Catalog* (Philadelphia: Jewish Publication Society, 1976), pp. 123–150.

31. N. Rabinovitch, "What is the *Halakhah* for Organ Transplants?" in *Tradition,* 1968, pp. 20–22.

32. Shulḥan Arukh, Yoreh Deah 339:1.

33. Rabbinical Council of America, Health Care Declaration (undated).

34. Pirkei Avot 5:24.

35. Kavesh, *op cit.*

36. Rabbinical Council of America, *op cit.*

37. Committee on Law and Standards, "Jewish Medical Directives for Healthcare," Rabbinical Assembly, 1993.

38. M. D. Tendler, "Care of the Critically Ill," *Responsa of Rav Moshe Feinstein,* Vol. 1 (KTAV, 1996), p. 47.

39. Elliot Dorff, *Matters of Life and Death* (Philadelphia: JPS, 1998), pp. 210 ff.

40. Genesis 21:15–16.

41. Exodus 16:3.

42. E. N. Dorff, *op. cit.* pp. 209–210.

43. Midrash Samuel 4 (ed. Buber, Cracow, 1903), p. 54.

Notes

44. B. Berakhot 56.

45. *The Guide of the Perplexed,* chapter 3.

46. See, for example, the second blessing of the Amida.

47. Presentation at the Rabbi Devora Bartnoff Memorial Conference on Judaism and Healing, Philadelphia, PA, April 28, 1998.

48. Elliot Dorff, *Matters of Life and Death: A Jewish Approach to Medical Ethics* (Philadelphia: JPS, 1998), p. 26.

49. P. Kiddushin 4:12 66d.

50. Leviticus Raba 34:1.

51. B. Nedarim.

52. *The Empty Chair* (Woodstock, VT: Jewish Lights, 1994), pp. 92–93.

53. Dorff, *op. cit.* pp. 205–207.

54. Shulḥan Arukh, Yoreh Deah 339:1.

55. Ecclesiastes Raba, 3:2, sec. 2.

56. Dorff, *op. cit.* pp. 199–200.

57. Commentary on Shulḥan Arukh Yoreh Deah 339:1 in Sefer Hasadim.

58. Yalkut Shimoni to Proverbs 943.

59. M. R. Billick, "Rethinking the Role of Tube Feeding in Patients with Advanced Dementia" in *New England Journal* 342:3, pp. 206–209.

60. Dorff, *op. cit.* pp. 208ff.

61. B. Ketubot 104a.

62. Kol Haneshamah prayer book series.

63. For example, B. Berakhot 5b.

64. Rabbi Dayle Friedman introduces this concept in *Jewish Pastoral Care: A Practical Handbook from Traditional and Contemporary Sources* (Woodstock, VT: Jewish Lights, 2000), pp. ix–xiii.

65. Peah 1:1.

66. B. Nedarim 40a.

67. Ibid.

68. B. Nedarim 39b.

69. Abrahams, *Hebrew Ethical Wills,* p. 40. Maimonides, Hilkhot Avelut 14:5.

70. Shulḥan Arukh 335:7.

71. *The Outstretched Arm,* Vol. III, No. 1, Fall 1993, p. 9.

72. There is a midrash that every living thing, even a blade of grass, has an angel who strikes it and commands, "Now is the time—grow!"

73. "Spiritual" refers to the deep inner realms of a person in which questions and apprehensions of ultimate meaning, connection, longing, and perception occur.

74. Saki Santorelli, *Heal Thyself: Lessons on Mindfulness in Medicine* (Bell Tower Books, 1999), p. 20.

75. See the *El Maley Raḥamim* prayer, which is said at the time of burial and in memorial services.

76. B. Berakhot.

77. Genesis 49:33.

78. See Avram Davis, *The Way of Flame* (HarperCollins), and Aryeh Kaplan, *Jewish Meditation: A Practical Guide* (Schocken Books).

79. *Kitzur Shulḥan Arukh: The Concise Book of Jewish Law.*

80. Ibid.

81. Macy Nulman, *The Encyclopedia of Jewish Prayer* (Jason Aronson Inc.).

82. See above.

83. See Myriam Klotz, "Jewish Healing Services" in *The Reconstructionist,* Spring 1999.

84. For assistance in constructing a healing circle, consult the National Center for Jewish Healing in New York City.

85. Levi Meier, *Jewish Values in Bioethics* (Human Sciences Press Inc.), pp. 28ff.

86. Sh'mot Raba 19.4.

87. See Chapter 8.

88. Likutey Moharan 4.5.

89. See Simcha Paull Raphael, *Jewish Views of the Afterlife* (Jason Aronson Press); Jack Riemer, editor, *Jewish Insights on Death and Mourning* (Schocken Books); and Maurice Lamm, *The Jewish Way in Death and Mourning* (Jonathan David Publisher).

90. Rabbi David ibn Zinma, the 16th-century Maimonidean commentator, cited by Rabbi David Bleich in "May One Refuse Medical Treatment?" in *Shma,* 23/443, December 11, 1992.

91. M. Semachot 1:4.

92. Maimonides, Mishneh Torah, Laws of Mourning, 4:5.

93. Cited in Louis E. Newman, *Past Imperatives: Studies in the History and Theory of Jewish Ethics* (Albany: State University of New York, 1998).

94. Tosafot to Avoda Zara 27b.

95. Proverbs 14:10, quoted in Yoma 83b.

96. Elliot N. Dorff, "A Jewish Approach to End-Stage Medical Care," in *Conservative Judaism,* Spring 1991, pp. 16–17.

97. See the discussion between Rabbis Elliot Dorff and Avram Reisner, as well as responses, in Aaron Mackler's *Life and Death Responsibilities in Jewish Biomedical Ethics* (New York: Jewish Theological Seminary, 2000), pp. 233–354.

98. Masekhet S'mahot 1; Shulḥan Arukh, Yoreh Deah 339.1.

99. Solomon B. Freehof, *American Reform Responsa,* Vol. LXXXV, No. 76, 1975.

100. Lamentations Raba 1:16 §51.

101. Noam Zohar, *Alternatives in Jewish Bioethics* (Albany: State University of New York Press, 1997).

102. In the three years from 1998 to 2000, 96 prescriptions were written under the Oregon law, and 70 people used such prescriptions to end their lives.

103. Ketubot 104a.

104. Shulḥan Arukh, Yoreh Deah 339.1.

105. Proverbs Raba 8.

106. Avoda Zara 18a.

107. In view of traditional Jewish strictures against cremation and prevailing contemporary sentiment in favor of burial, throughout this guide "burial" is used as the normal referent for the final disposition of the body. An extended discussion of issues and options with regard to the choice of cremation is on page 178.

INDEX